PICTORIAL HISTORY
OF THE ROYAL NAVY

PICTORIAL HISTORY
OF THE
Royal Navy

ANTHONY J. WATTS

VOLUME TWO · 1880–1914

LONDON
IAN ALLAN

First published 1971

SBN 7110 0243 6

*Published by Ian Allan Ltd, Shepperton, Surrey, and printed in
Great Britain by Morrison and Gibb Ltd, London and Edinburgh*

Contents

Foreword

IN THIS SECOND VOLUME of the *Pictorial History of the Royal Navy* the development of the navy from 1880 to 1914 is described. The race to build larger and more powerful warships, the improvements in machinery, and the changeover of gunnery from being an art to one of being a science; these and the personality conflicts and the rise of the German navy form the main points of historical interest during this period.

At the turn of the century the Royal Navy was the largest and most impressive in the world. Queen Victoria was on the throne and the pomp and circumstance was unequalled. All this majesty and grandeur had its effect on the navy. Every year there was a Review of the Fleet, when line upon line of battleships stretched as far as the eye could see. Hundreds of yachts decorated with bunting dashed hither and thither: all the brasswork on the warships gleamed in the sunlight, and officers marched proudly round their charges in white uniforms. The bands played, while elegantly dressed ladies and their consorts waltzed on the quarterdeck.

From 1880 to 1914 the navy and its ships and our men were the envy of all the world. The First World War was soon to change all the splendour and gay life. The ships were to be stripped of their beautiful teak woodwork, no more balls would be held on board, and all the polish would dull. Life would never be quite the same again. From being a peacekeeping force, policing the oceans, the navy had to transform its ships and men into highly complex machines, capable of taking on any force in the world.

It was hard to discard the gay social life, but it was accepted and the Royal Navy went to war supremely confident in its ability to outclass the German Navy.

As with Volume I it has been impossible to include, in such a concise work as this, all the points of historical interest connected with the navy over this period, and if by some omission I have offended any reader it is completely unintentional.

I should like to extend my thanks to all those who have assisted me in the preparation of this book, and especially to Miss L. Boutroy of the Mansell Collection and to Miss Shepherd of the Radio Times Hulton Picture Library. I should also like to acknowledge the assistance of the photographic staff of the National Maritime Museum and the Imperial War Museum, and also to Mr. P. Vicary for the many interesting photographs which they have found for me. Finally I should like to thank my father for checking the manuscript for grammatical errors and my wife for all the help and encouragement she has given me during my research for this work.

Introduction

THE GOLDEN AGE of British Industrialism had a marked effect on the Royal Navy. Steel was now established as the main constructional metal in the shipping industry, first being used to any great extent in the *Comus* Class cruisers. Machinery too, under the aegis of the Industrial Revolution, was making great strides forward, but not without its problems. Like many other spheres of life the majority of men in the navy tended to be conservative and these new "fangled" machines were looked upon with awe, wonderment, suspicion, fear and incredulity. Gradually, however, steam engines came to be accepted as the mode of propulsion. But practically up to the end of the century there were still vessels with steam and sail on the active lists, and even the shore establishments trained men in the art of sailing ships.

The period from 1880 to 1914 was one of consolidation and relaxation for the Royal Navy. The great changes wrought as a result of the Industrial Revolution were almost complete. The steam engine and its boilers were greatly improved and slowly the engineers who operated them came to be accepted by their brother officers and men. Protection was also improved, new processes for the production of armour plate giving warships greater strength. This meant that improved guns had to be designed to penetrate armour. The race between gun and armour reached its height during this period, with new guns being produced almost yearly. At long last a satisfactory breech mechanism was devised and the gun at once began to improve, especially as new constructional methods greatly increased the strength of the barrel and more powerful explosives to fire the shell were produced.

The art of gunnery itself, however, lapsed dismally. On the whole the Victorian Navy did not look upon guns with favour. Like the steam engines before them, they were viewed with disfavour as firing them made an awful noise and the ships took hours to clean after a shoot. In many cases Battle practices were a farce, the range being kept far too low, and no real effort made to improve the efficiency. The intention was to get the exercise over as quickly as possible so that the ship could return to port, show the flag again, and continue the gay social life. There were some, however, who did not enjoy indulging in all the social functions which were a feature of the Victorian navy. Very gradually under the guidance of a dedicated few, who many regarded as cranks, the efficiency of the navy was improved.

The Empire was then at its zenith and the small gunboats and cruisers in the Royal Navy were busy keeping the peace. The only real actions were minor skirmishes in the Far East, where pirates and rebellions still caused trouble, and on the continent of Africa, where British interests came into conflict with other European Powers. No longer was Britain calling the tune. Other countries had to be taken into consideration, and one in particular was becoming more and more aggressive in its attitude.

France had always been regarded as Britain's natural enemy, but almost imperceptibly the situation was changed as the two countries found themselves more and more in accord over their views of the international situation, and especially with regards to Germany.

At long last the country realised that German intentions were not quite so peaceful as they at first seemed. The German Navy Laws could have only one purpose—to challenge the might of the Royal Navy. At first only a few farsighted men realised that these Laws posed such a dire threat to the Royal Navy's supremacy at sea. Under the guidance of these men, and one in particular, Admiral Fisher, our own navy was completely reorganised and, more important, new warships were designed to combat the Kaiser's Fleet.

The British government's of the day were unwilling to spend vast sums of money on the navy, as they were busily engaged in carrying out expensive programmes of social reform aimed at relieving the hardships of many at home. Finally, after much argument, the government was convinced of the German threat and new ships were designed and built. Matters had been left dangerously late, and when war broke out in 1914 the navy was only just ready to engage in the new conflict. Even so there were deficiencies, but these were not to show themselves until the war was well under way.

CHAPTER I

Economy and the Royal Navy

Great expense is involved in naval matters
CICERO

WITH THE CONSTRUCTION of the *Comus* class cruisers well under way it was decided that a new class of protected cruiser, known as the *Amphion* class, should be laid down. The first of these, the *Arethusa*, was laid down in 1880 and followed by three others. Although the displacement was only 4300 tons the class was fitted with ten 6in guns, and very soon gained a reputation for being overgunned. On top of this they proved to be inferior sea boats, but managed to maintain their speed well.

In the meantime the Admiralty was conducting experiments with a view to reintroducing the breech-loading gun into the navy. Improvements to the muzzle velocities and penetration powers of guns had been dictated by the advancements in armour made during the previous decade. As a result of the experiments it was found that to achieve greater muzzle velocity a slow-burning large-grain powder was necessary. This new powder gave increased pressure in the gun barrel when ignited and gave the shell the extra speed required without increasing the weight and bore of the gun. However, the use of the new powder in the old muzzle-loading guns was unsatisfactory, the shell often leaving the muzzle before the charge was completely burnt. It was decided, therefore, to increase the length of the gun barrel. This meant loading the guns from outside the turrets, as in the *Inflexible* (SEE VOL. I PAGE 56), a method which proved unsatisfactory. Therefore in 1879 a Committee had been appointed to investigate the possibilities of again using the breech-loading gun in HM warships. The main fault of the earlier breech-loading guns was that the breech failed to close properly. In the new model, designed by the firm of Elswick, the French idea of fitting automatic safety devices to the breech was adopted. The mechanism prevented the gun from being fired until the interrupted-screw action had locked. The new weapon was offered to the Admiralty, but before it was finally accepted a number of experiments were conducted. While these were in progress a group of naval officers were sent to Germany to witness trials of a new Krupp breech-loading gun. As a result of the report on the Krupp trials it was immediately decided to order breech-loading guns for all future British warships. The War Office, up to that time responsible for all the ordnance of the navy, at once ordered designs of 12in breech-loading guns from the works at Woolwich and Armstrongs. The Woolwich design was finally approved in February 1882. Details of the charge and shell, however, were not completed until March 1884. This was not the only dangerous delay in the designing of the new guns, for the methods and materials used in their construction were also at fault. This was first realised in 1880, but very little was done about it until November 1886, when Captain J. A. Fisher was appointed Director of Naval Ordnance and rectified the faults. Following the appointment of Captain Fisher a campaign was begun for the navy to assume responsibility for its own ordnance and ammunition, matters previously dealt with by the War Office. Under the old system all the navy's guns and ammunition had been pooled with those of the army, and the army was always given priority when it came to ordering new weapons and ammunition.

While all the arguments were in progress over the new guns a new class of battleships had been laid down. The new vessels—called the *Collosus* and *Edinburgh*—were to all intents and purposes sister ships to the *Agamemnon*. They were designed to mount four muzzle-loading guns, but as soon as the design for the new 12in gun was approved in 1882, it was decided to fit these. In addition to the new breech-loading guns the *Collosus* and *Edinburgh* were fitted with two 14in torpedo tubes. Steel was used in the general construction and all the armour was of the compound type, instead of iron as hitherto. The new 12in guns had an unfortunate start to their life when one being used in trials in the *Collingwood* burst, in May 1886, due to faulty materials. At the time the *Collosus* was nearing completion, and to avoid any possible mishaps the commanding officer was ordered not to fire his new 12in guns until they had been removed and modified.

Throughout the 1880s France was still regarded by Britain as the potential enemy. With the French *Formidable* class battleships mounting three 75-ton breech-loading guns newly commissioned, and the *Caiman*, a super coast-defence battleship entering service, the Admiralty felt the need for a vessel to counter this impending threat. The First Sea Lord, Admiral Sir George Wellesley, ordered a design to be prepared for a vessel not larger than 10000 tons. This limit on the displacement meant that the warship would be no better than a second-class coast-defence vessel and would certainly not be superior to the larger French and Italian vessels then under construction. The final design plans for the vessel were left in the hands of Barnaby's assistant, W. H. White. The Controller of the navy, Vice-Admiral Sir William Houstan Stewart, recommended that a new mark of the 12in breech-loader should be mounted in the vessel, which had been given the name *Collingwood*. In addition to this, Vice-Admiral Stewart proposed that the 12in guns should be mounted in a barbette, instead of the more normal turret. The barbette system of mounting had certain advantages over the turret. The guns could be mounted much higher than in a turret because the mounting was far lighter and elevation and depression were not restricted as in a turret. The echelon positioning used with the turrets in the *Collosus* was dispensed with and the barbettes of the *Collingwood* mounted fore and aft on the keel line. The compound armour protection was concentrated in a short heavy waterline belt 8 to 18in thick amidships, protecting both engines, boilers and communication tubes of the barbettes. The ends of the armour belt were closed by bulkheads 16in thick, the whole being covered by a protective deck, flat over the armoured belt and slightly curved fore and aft. The *Collingwood* proved to be an excellent design, her only fault being the low freeboard, which with her high speed of 16 knots meant that mobility in a seaway was considerably impaired. With the *Collingwood* the navy at last crystallised its ideas on the development of the battleship and all succeeding classes were really improvements and modifications of the *Collingwood* design. Future development differed in this respect from the previous two decades where there were numerous separate designs, each emphasising some particular aspect such as the ram bow, guns, turrets, etc.

In 1880, Gladstone had again taken office as Prime Minister with the First Earl of Northbrook, Thomas George Baring, as the First Lord and Admiral Sir Cooper Key, KCB, as First Sea Lord. Not for the first, or the last time, did an administration prove to be so unpopular after an extended term of service. Lord Northbrook had an obsession with economy, and did everything in his power to keep the service estimates as low as possible, often being unintentionally aided by members of the Board of Admiralty who could not decide on the type of warship that they should construct, thus delaying construction, or designing vessels which caused much criticism within the service. As a start to reducing expenditure it was planned to pay off large numbers of ships, discharge many workmen from the dockyards and to cease purchasing stores. The trend had been set by a previous First Lord—Hugh Childers (SEE VOL. I PAGE 50), and Gladstone happily continued the process of whittling away the navy until it was not even strong enough to meet any possible opposition that the French Fleet might offer. The Board of Admiralty was finally forced to order some second class ships for overseas service, and to increase the rate of construction, which in the case of the *Ajax* and *Collingwood*, was being seriously delayed, the vessels finally taking seven years to complete. Apart from these difficulties there was also the problems of guns and sails! This matter had still not been resolved in the minds of certain members of the Board of Admiralty, and the new disposition of breech-loading guns created problems with the mounting, and handling of sails. The new Administration was convinced of the economy of using sails whenever possible, instead of costly coal, and as a result of this a design was prepared which developed into the *Imperieuse* and *Warspite*, the last armoured warships to be designed for the Royal Navy with a square rig. For armament they carried four 9.2in guns of a new design which were sited in single mountings fore and aft and amidships to port and starboard (the gun disposition adopted in French warships), the only British vessels to so carry their armament. It was felt that such a placing of the guns would give the vessels a tremendous advantage in any cruiser action. Another unique feature of the ships was their tumblehome sides, again a design feature of French warships and unknown in the British navy. They were described in Parliament as "amongst the most complete failures of modern warships; badly designed; badly carried out; and absolutely dangerous".

Following the large French programme of construction begun in 1880, the Board of Admiralty set about ordering new vessels for the navy. They were undecided, however, as to what type of ship they should order. Finally a class of four ships very similar to the *Collingwood*, then still under construction, was ordered. Together with the *Collingwood*, and later the *Benbow*, this class—the *Anson*, *Camperdown*, *Howe* and *Rodney*, came to be known as the *Admirals*. By the time the four vessels were laid down the more powerful 13.5in gun had been designed and it was decided that the class should mount the new gun. Being slightly heavier than the 12in, the 13.5in would put the second group of *Admirals* on a par with recently completed French ships. Delays in the production of the 13.5 gun, and certain faults in the guns themselves which had to be eradicated before the ships could mount the weapon, meant that the second group of *Admirals* did not finally enter service until the end of the decade. A repeat order for a fifth ship, the *Benbow*, followed, and in an attempt to hurry construction it was decided to try and find an alternative to the 13.5in gun. The only other gun available was a new Elswick designed 16.25in. This was duly fitted, but its great increase in weight over the 13.5in (110 tons as against

67 tons) meant that only one could be mounted in each barbette instead of two. Although the new gun enabled the *Benbow* to be completed before any of her sister ships, in itself the 16.25in was not as satisfactory as the 13.5in, being much slower in operation and with a much shorter life.

TABLE 1

Comparison of main armament of 1880

Ship	Cal	Length	Weight	Weight of projectile	Muzzle velocity	Muzzle energy	Penetration of compound armour at 2000yd
Inflexible	16in ML	18-cal	81 tons	1684lb	1590ft/sec	29530ft-tons	15in
Benbow	16.25in BL	30-cal	110 tons	1800lb	2148ft/sec	57580ft-tons	19in
Anson	13.5in BL	30-cal	67 tons	1250lb	2025ft/sec	35560ft-tons	17in
Majestic	12in BL	35-cal	46 tons	850lb	2367ft/sec	33940ft-tons	
Colossus	12in BL	25-cal	45 tons	714lb	2000ft/sec	18060ft-tons	12½in
Imperieuse	9.2in BL	25-cal	22 tons	380lb	1809ft/sec	8622ft-tons	10in

Egypt had for many years seethed with discontent. A contributory cause was the bankruptcy in 1876 of the Khedive Ismail Pasha, ruler of Egypt. During the 1860s the French had completed the Suez Canal, which at once proved of inestimable value, the long sea journey round the Cape of Good Hope in South Africa no longer being necessary to reach the French Empire in the Far East. It also proved of great value to the British who were able to use the short route to get to India. With both Britain and France vying for influence in Egypt the bankruptcy of the Khedive at last forced a rapprochement between the two countries. Combining forces under the leadership of Lord Salisbury, who was determined not to allow the French to get the advantage of the situation, the two countries at once set about the problem of recovering the money necessary to settle Egypt's debts, and an International Commission of the Public Debt was formed to collect this money. In effect this meant that the Egyptians were placed under Anglo-French rule. Taxes were imposed which infuriated both the ruling classes and the peasants. Arising from the resulting discontent many nationalist cells formed in order to overthrow the foreign administration. Finally in 1881 the Egyptian army under Arabi Pasha took control of the Administration of the country. By this time Gladstone had become Prime Minister and not wishing to release the British hold on the Suez Canal he agreed to the sending of a joint British-French note to Arabi Pasha. The note, sent in January 1882, failed to have the necessary impact, and Arabi Pasha, inferring that armed intervention was hinted at in the note, began building up the fortifications of Alexandria. This act of provocation failed to stir the Allies, who waited until May before sending a combined squadron of warships. With such a powerful force outside Alexandria the Khedive Tewfik Pasha, son of Ismail Pasha, was persuaded to dismiss Arabi Pasha, but so strong was the anti British-French feeling throughout the country that five days later he was back in office.

The last straw was a reported massacre of Europeans. At this Gladstone instructed Admiral Sir Frederick Beauchamp Seymour to send an ulti-matum to Arabi Pasha. Admiral Seymour, being rather overzealous, de-manded that Arabi Pasha disarm his forts or else be bombarded. By this time the French had withdrawn their warships from the squadron and Admiral Seymour was forced to act on his own. The squadron was com-prised of a mixture of sail, steam, iron and wooden vessels, representative of all the major types of warship then in the Royal Navy, including eight battleships (the most modern being the *Inflexible* with Captain J. A. Fisher in command), three gunvessels (including the *Condor* under command of Commander Lord Charles Beresford) and two gunboats.

The squadron took up its pre-arranged bombarding position on the evening of July 10. At 0700 the following morning the bombardment began, a number of the forts soon being heavily damaged. Tactically the attack was an unfortunate error as not only did it fail to subdue Arabi Pasha but brought the whole of Egypt into open revolt. This forced Gladstone to send in the army, who gradually restored the situation, until Egypt's rich protectorate—the Sudan—broke into revolt under the leadership of the Mahdi. The Egyptian Army sent to repress the rebellion was wiped out and to cover British possessions on the Red Sea Coast a squadron under Rear-Admiral Sir William Hewett was sent to the area.

As a result of the debacle in Egypt, British Foreign Policy underwent a change which was to have its effect on the navy, not least on the small gun-boats which were often instrumental in carrying out Foreign Policy. The Empire began to wane and almost imperceptibly Britain's isolated position was undermined, as at ever more frequent intervals she was forced to enter into diplomatic negotiations with other European Powers.

By the 1880s the problem of *matériel* had become a vital question in the navy, and in recognition of its importance the Controller was made a member of the Board of Admiralty. This change was instituted in 1882 when Rear-Admiral Thomas Brandreth was appointed Controller. At the same time another important post was created, that of Civil Lord, who was to assist the Controller and who had not only to be an administrative assistant but also a qualified engineer. To fill this new post the Admiralty appointed George Rendel of Armstrong's. Apart from this, however, little was done to increase the *matériel* strength of the navy during the early 1880s. The fleet was still a motley collection of hybrid vessels, very few of which could operate together as a homogeneous squadron. Submarines, although in the early stages of development, were thought to be an ungentlemanly weapon and rather impracticable. The voices of criticism were few and far between and the general public knew very little of the real state of the navy and its weaknesses. In July 1884 Lord Sidmouth drew attention to this poor state of affairs in the House of Lords, and asked that the Admiralty be given unlimited funds to build a new navy. Lord Northbrook replied for the Admiralty making a most unfortunate statement—"The great difficulty the Admiralty would have to contend with, if they were granted three or four millions tomorrow for the purpose referred to, would be to decide how they should spend the money . . . Then there was another consideration, which made it doubtful whether it would be wise to spend a great sum of money now upon such ships. (Ships with greater armour for protection against more powerful guns—author's note.) Some of the finest naval officers in Britain thought that, in the event of another war the torpedo would be the most powerful weapon of offence . . . Then it would be most imprudent greatly to increase the number of these enormous machines". This reply was completely misconstrued by the general public who gained the impression that Lord Northbrook regarded the navy as having adequate strength and that no more money was required. What Lord Northbrook meant, in fact, was that with the apparent inability of large ships to defend themselves against attack by torpedo craft, the sudden expenditure of vast sums of money on these vessels would probably be wasted. In fact the only defence against the torpedo at the time appeared to be the torpedo net, which was slung out from long wooden booms strung high above the waterline. Experiments had proved that these nets could stop a 14in torpedo, but there was every possibility that the torpedo would explode and blow a large hole in the net, rendering it useless. Edward Reed then put forward an idea that he thought would provide an effective defence against torpedo attack. It consisted of giving a warship an armoured bottom with a thin outer shell that would be divided transversely and longitudinally. The armoured bottom was to run under the magazines, boilers and machinery. This method of construction would raise the level of the machinery, exposing it to the destructive effect of shellfire which might penetrate the belt. Unfortunately the Admiralty calculated that if a torpedo should breach six compartments in the bottom, after both ends of the vessel had been flooded, then there was a danger she might capsize. (Such a system of construction was used in the Japanese *Yamato* class battleships of 1937 and *Musashi* took 19 torpedo hits and 17 bombs before sinking in 1944 in an identical situation such as was envisaged by the Admiralty.)

With a General Election in the offing in the Autumn of 1884 it was decided to print a series of articles on the navy in the Liberal paper the *Pall Mall Gazette*. The Hon. Reginald Brett and Captain J. A. Fisher, commanding officer of the gunnery school *Excellent*, supplied the editor of the magazine, W. T. Stead, with all the information necessary to write the articles. When printed the series of articles completely damned the Board of Admiralty and the Government, showing the navy to be utterly deficient in men, organisation, ships, stores and equipment. As a result of the outcry that followed the publication of the articles, Lord Northbrook was forced to institute a programme of reform and new construction. This programme of construction, of armoured warships and cruisers, was vital to the well being of Britain, as by this time much of the food and materials for industry were being imported and the navy was responsible for the protection of this trade. The estimates for 1884 voted an additional £3.1m for a five-year plan of construction which included the *Sans Pareil*, *Victoria*, seven cruisers of the *Australia* class, six torpedo cruisers of the *Archer* class and fourteen torpedo boats. The Admiralty covered its previous failings by saying that if a similar programme had been instituted before, there would have been such an outcry from the public that the Estimates would never have been passed. They also said that as the feelings of the public had now been aroused in favour of the expenditure, it was in fact adequate.

While the details of the new programme were being worked out the Admiralty ordered two second class torpedo boats from Thornycroft, who had just perfected a new type of boiler. This was the water tube boiler, and to test its capacities *No. 99*, fitted with the old type of locomotive boiler, was tested against *No. 100*, fitted with the new boiler. The main advantage of the water-tube boiler was its greater heating surface compared to the locomotive boiler (606sq ft as against $265\frac{1}{2}$sq ft). The working pressure was increased from 130 to 145lb and on trials torpedo boat *No. 100* made 16.81 knots compared with the 16.13 knots of *No. 99*. In spite of the success of the trials, the Admiralty were slow to see the possibilities of the new boiler and not until the following decade was any move made to adopt it in HM ships.

On top of all its administrative problems the Admiralty was suddenly faced with the prospect of a war when relations with Russia deteriorated. The scare blew up when Russia invaded Bulgaria and Afghanistan and then gave an ultimatum that she also required India as a political necessity. The Government prepared for war and the Admiralty called out the Reserves, at the same time taking over the island of Port Hamilton south of Korea as an advanced base for warships. All Russian ships were shadowed by an equal British force. In June 1885 a Special Service Squadron was formed to constitute the Baltic Expeditionary Fleet under Admiral Sir Phipps Hornby. The squadron was a diverse collection of obsolete warships none of which was suitable for such an operation. Many months passed before some of the vessels were ready for service, and some had not even finished fitting out when the scare eventually passed. As the situation eased it was decided to complete the mobilisation of the squadron and then to keep it together as the Particular Service Squadron, employing it in exercises to test sea going qualities and the value of the new torpedo boats, nets, mines, etc.

The *Sans Pareil* and *Victoria* laid down under the 1884 Programme (SEE ABOVE) carried the development of the battleship one stage further by being fitted with the new triple expansion engines. The horsepower developed was the same as in the *Admiral* class, but the number of boilers was reduced from twelve to eight and the working pressure raised from 90lb to 135lb. The general design, however, was misguided, being based on the earlier *Conqueror*, but with the proviso that they were to be sea-going vessels. They had a distinctive silhouette with the funnel and bridge aft and a massive turret forward mounting two 16.25in guns, whose delivery was yet again delayed, holding up completion of the vessels.

At the time the *Mersey* class protected cruisers, named after British rivers, were laid down. Four vessels were commenced in 1883 to an Admiralty design, the Chief Constructor, Barnaby, being given the specifications around which to plan the class. Like many other vessels built at this time the *Mersey*'s quickly became obsolescent on the introduction of the quick-firing gun. Following this the battleships *Nile* and *Trafalgar* were ordered under the 1886 Estimates. Before the designs had been agreed, however, Gladstone resigned. Lord Salisbury again became Prime Minister and appointed Lord George Hamilton as First Lord, with Admiral Sir Arthur Hood as First Sea Lord. To appease public agitation over the state of the navy a Fourth Sea Lord, Lord Charles Beresford, was created, and plans were drawn up for reforming the navy. Before commencing any material reconstruction a complete reorganisation had to be undertaken and great changes were made in the administration of the navy and the dockyards. The previous years of financial shortcomings had wrought havoc with the state of the navy and Lord Beresford prepared a memorandum on this aspect putting forward proposals for the formation of a War Staff, which were rejected by the Board of Admiralty as being unnecessary. At this Lord Beresford showed his plans to Lord Salisbury, who at once set about having a Naval Intelligence Department formed on the strength of Lord Beresford's arguments.

This new Board of Admiralty was the last of its type to be formed, all future Boards being purely naval appointments made by the War Office (except that is, the post of First Lord—a civil post). The Chief Constructor Barnaby resigned his post at this time as he no longer saw eye to eye with the Board in matters of design and his post was filled by Mr. White, the post of assistant previously held by George Rendel being dispensed with when White was appointed. In the reorganisation the First Lord had all Lord Northbrook's plans scrapped, except for the designs of the *Nile* and *Trafalgar*, and even these were recast to his own specifications. During construction of the *Nile* and *Trafalgar* certain modifications were incorporated into the vessels to such an extent that when completed the upper edge of the citadel was only 9½ft above the waterline instead of the 11ft designed. This brought to light a dangerous practise that had been carried out in dockyards for many years, that of adding extra equipment to vessels after the design had been passed. Many vessels had had their displacements so increased and often to a really dangerous degree. As a result the Board of Admiralty introduced the 4% margin which allowed all future designs a leeway on the designed displacement so that such additions or alterations could be made with safety. One of the additions made to the *Nile* class was in the secondary armament, where instead of the 5in planned, a new Elswick 4.7in QF gun was fitted. The quick-firing gun now became the standard secondary armament for battleships, going a long way towards providing an antidote for the torpedo boat. The new 4.7in gun had great range and accuracy and also a high rate of fire (one round every eight seconds).

Before all these new programmes of construction could be undertaken, however, the new developments in torpedoes, guns, and explosives had to be thoroughly investigated. To keep pace with the advances in armament and protection, the old ironclad *Resistance* was fitted with special armour plates and commissioned as a target ship. She was then subjected to shell-fire from the new guns, explosives and torpedoes. These experiments continued for some years, the Admiralty gaining much from the results. One of the trials showed that the power of a 14in torpedo was far less than the Admiralty had been led to believe. To increase the charge the size was increased first to 15in and later to 18in, the speed and range remaining virtually the same as in the 14in.

In 1887 the Colonial Conference published extracts from a report prepared by the Carnarvon Commission. This Royal Commission had been formed in 1879 to investigate and report on "The Defence of British possessions and commerce abroad". The report was like a thunderbolt. The defences of overseas bases were practically non-existent. Hong Kong and Singapore had none, while the remainder were so weak that they would never have stood up to a determined attack from the sea. This was not all, for the report also said that in its present state the navy would be incapable of defending the sea lanes or the bases. The vessels at present stationed overseas were largely the slow and lightly armed gunboats, and were quite unequal to the task expected of them in those times. To complete the picture the report summed up by saying that the navy was not even prepared for its new duties of commerce protection. The 1886–1887 Estimates, for example, only provided for small weakly armed cruisers, incapable of fighting in heavy seas, and a number of sloops, which had been ordered in addition to the experimental torpedo boat *Sharpshooter*.

Consequent upon this report Mr. White outlined to the Admiralty in 1888 his plans for new construction, and a list of 72 vessels that he proposed to scrap as obsolete. Covering the four years 1889–1892 this plan formed the basis of the Naval Defence Act of 1889. The Admiralty could not bring themselves to authorise the scrapping of so many vessels and the only ships deleted from the lists between 1889 and 1894 were the *Defence*, *Hector*, *Valiant* and the *Warrior*, eight wooden cruisers, eight wooden sloops and ten gun vessels. The remaining "obsolete" vessels were reboilered and modernised. The vast programme of construction, which was to cost £21.5m, allowed for the construction of seven *Royal Sovereign* class battleships, the battleship *Hood*, two *Centurion* second-class battleships, nine *Edgar* first-class cruisers, eight *Astrea* class cruisers, 21 *Apollo* second-class cruisers, four *Pallas* third-class crusiers and 18 *Sharpshooter* type torpedo gunboats.

The Admiralty also ordered that Annual Manoeuvres be conducted from 1888 onwards, during which a partial mobilisation of the Fleet would be carried out. Unfortunately the manoeuvres were not at first as valuable as might have been hoped, for many of the exercises and movements were designed more with an eye for competition between ships than as a serious preparation for war. The gunnery exercises were looked on by many officers with distaste as they made a fearful mess of the vessels, and cleanliness was the epitomy of the Victorian navy.

To study all the aspects of the exercises a Committee was appointed with the special instruction to look at the feasibility of blockading an enemy squadron in its home port. Special importance was placed on the ratios of capital ships and cruisers of the blockading and blockaded fleets, the possibility of keeping watch on the blockaded fleet by fast cruisers while the main battlefleet remained at home, or the possibility of keeping the battle squadron off the enemy port, supported by an inshore squadron. Apart from these important considerations the Committee was also asked to note "The value of torpedo gunboats and first-class torpedo boats both with the blockading and blockaded Fleets, and the most efficient manner of utilising them". In addition the qualities of various new vessels in the Royal Navy were also to be studied.

During the early part of 1889 the report on the 1888 manoeuvres was presented to Parliament, and the content severely criticised the performance of various vessels and most important of all laid down the principle of British Sea Power, maintaining the absolute necessity for adhering to a Two Power Standard. In addition the report stated that in its present state the Royal Navy was incapable of even engaging in an offensive war with one nation let alone two! To maintain an effective blockade, said the report, a superiority of at least 5 to 3 was necessary and preferably greater. If, however, an anchorage near to the blockaded port was suitable, the superiority need only be 4 to 3, but the blockading Fleet would need to be very well supported in such an instance. Torpedo boats as an adjunct to a blockading force were dismissed as being of little value, although they might be of some use to the blockaded fleet. Torpedo gunboats, like the *Rattlesnake*, were thought to be ideal for blockading purposes.

On the basis of this report the Admiralty commenced reforms which were to effect the whole state of the navy.

CHAPTER 2

The Naval Defence Act

*The Royal Navy of England hath ever been its greatest
defence and ornament, it is its ancient and natural
strength, the floating bulwark of our island*
SIR WILLIAM BLACKSTONE

THE PROBLEMS and difficulties which faced the Royal Navy during the
1890s were many and varied. On the question of welfare there was still
much ground to be made. Training methods were also antiquated. The
seamanship of both officers and men was still initially done on board sailing
vessels, and life on the lower deck was still hard. The ordinary seaman was
looked upon as a rather unintelligent creature with primitive habits. At
meal times they ate their food with their fingers as cutlery was regarded as
an unnecessary expense for these men. Improvements had been made with
the victualling, and rations were more varied, but they were poorly prepared and cooked. In spite of these hardships the morale of the navy was
high.

Africa during the 1890s was to cause the British Government many a
headache. Already Britain and France were beginning to be at variance
over their defined spheres of influence in the continent, and the race for
colonisation began.

Egypt and her difficulties were at the root of the trouble and in the
1890s Britain was forced to make certain colonial concessions in Africa and
the Pacific in order to obtain German approval for her policies in Egypt,
and South Africa. Trouble first became apparent in West Africa, where the
French, no longer passive in that part of the continent, began to exploit
trading possibilities on the lower Niger and Congo Rivers. The lower
Niger was looked upon as a British domain, and the French were offered
Senegal and the Upper Niger in return for their quiescence, but they
refused. On the Congo, the British countered the French move by
recognising Portuguese claims to the area, hoping the Portuguese would
look after the area on behalf of the British. Again the French refused to be

21

intimidated, and opened negotiations with the Germans. Without German support on the International Debt Commission (SEE PAGE 13), British efforts to rule Egypt were doomed to failure, so the proposed British/Portuguese Treaty over the Congo proved to be abortive.

Following her retreat in West Africa, Britain was forced to concede certain parts of East Africa (opposite the island of Zanzibar), to Germany. This was to store up trouble for Britain in the future. The Portuguese followed by making moves on the Zambesi River, hoping to use it as a route to Central Africa. This was too much, and in 1889 the gunboat *Stork* was sent to the River to show the flag, surveying the mouth of the Zambesi at the same time.

In 1890 Lord Salisbury at last asserted British rights. A small squadron composed of the *Herald*, *Mosquito*, *Pigeon* and *Redbreast* was assembled with a view to intimidating the Portuguese. The *Pigeon* and *Redbreast* crossed the bar at the mouth of the river and forced their way upstream. The *Pigeon* soon returned owing to the difficulties of navigation and the possible loss of the vessels. The *Redbreast* continued upstream finally breaking out into the open river, whereon the Portuguese capitulated, recognising British claims to the lakes. Thereafter the *Herald* and *Mosquito* being stern-wheel gunboats built especially for working on the Zambesi patrolled the lakes.

The following year (1891) found the British and French in dispute over their boundaries in West Africa. The French fomented tribal unrest in the area of the Gambia River and the *Alecto*, *Swallow* and *Widgeon* concentrated on the river and landed a number of sailors to restore peace. A further show of force was required at the end of 1891, and this time the *Sparrow*, *Thrush* and *Widgeon* landed men. By the end of January 1892 nearly 500 men were engaged in the operation which came to an end the following month, when it was learned that the tribal chief responsible for the uprising had fled over the border to seek asylum in French territory.

Following the plans laid down for the new Defence Act (SEE PAGE 19), Mr. White was ordered to draw up a design for a new battleship. Certain improvements were built into the ships, and included raising the freeboard and mounting the guns two feet higher than in the *Trafalgar*, upon which the design was based. The secondary battery was to be increased to ten of the new 6in quick-firers and a large number of 3-pdr and machine guns were to be carried. Owing to the conflict of ideas upon the positioning of armour between Mr. White and the First Sea Lord, Admiral Hood, the final design was a compromise between the second group of *Admiral*'s and the *Trafalgar* design. This was affected mainly as a result of certain improvements suggested in 1889 by the armour producing firm of Jessops at Sheffield. The improvements allowed for a greater proportion of the sides to be covered with armour plate without any increase in displacement. The armour was an alloy of nickel-steel and proved extremely hard and durable compared to other types of armour. The greater tensile strength of the new armour meant that to achieve the same protection as earlier vessels, the 20in compound armour of the *Trafalgar* could be reduced to 18in of nickel-steel. Seven vessels were ordered to the new design, known as the *Royal Sovereign* class. Four 13.5in guns were mounted in barbettes instead of turrets and the secondary armament was increased to ten 6in QF. The four 6in on the main deck were mounted in casemates instead of in the open as hitherto, and the remainder were given plain shields. In addition sixteen 6-pdr QF were carried together with twelve 3-pdr QF. The main feature of the *Royal Sovereign*'s was an extra deck, which gave the vessels a high freeboard greatly improving sea-keeping qualities and enabling high speeds to be maintained in heavy seas. To help any tendency to instability arising from the extra deck, the sides of the hull had a distinctive tumblehome.

An eighth ship of the class was ordered, but she differed in a number of ways from the earlier vessels. The main distinguishing feature was the gun mounting. White was very much in favour of the barbette to which the First Sea Lord was strongly opposed. As a gesture in recognition of Admiral Hood's feelings, White planned that the new vessel, named *Hood* after the First Sea Lord, should be completed with turrets. The extra deck of the *Royal Sovereign*'s was omitted in this vessel and the guns were only 17ft above the waterline. As a result, the *Hood* lacked the good sea-keeping qualities of the earlier vessels and her stability was poor. It was so poor in fact, that the designers were forced to dispense with the casemates for the 6in guns as they would have brought the centre of gravity to a dangerous level.

In March 1889 the Controller requested plans for two second-class battleships with a draught not exceeding 26ft, for use on the rivers of the Far East. The specified radius of action was 6000 miles (the same as that of the *Imperieuse*) for which an estimated bunkerage of not more than 750 tons was to be provided. For reasons of economy the price was kept as low as possible, forcing the displacement to be reduced by 4000 tons. As a result the vessels could only mount 10in and 4.7in for their armament and protection had to be greatly reduced. The *Barfleur* and *Centurion*—as the vessels were named—were notable for the fact that the barbettes for the 10in guns were fitted with an armoured hood, and they could be loaded with the barbettes trained in any direction. In an effort to reduce weight, the barbettes were circular in shape, as opposed to earlier mountings which had all been "pear-shaped". Training was achieved either by steam or hand, the steam proving unsatisfactory in service as it failed to stop the turret quickly enough. All future ships were thus fitted with hydraulic gear. Although only designed to carry 750 tons of coal, under service conditions, the vessels actually carried a maximum of 1125 tons giving them a radius of action of 9750 miles. A speed of 18½ knots was made on a forced draught of 13000hp, 1½ knots more than the *Royal Sovereign*'s. In spite of the fact that they were only rated as second-class battleships, the *Barfleur* and *Centurion* were quite powerful vessels and can be considered as the forerunners of the battlecruiser, where a ship carried fewer guns of slightly smaller calibre than a battleship at a higher speed and with rather less protection.

TABLE 2

	Royal Sovereign	Centurion
Displacement	14100 tons	10500 tons
Horsepower	13000	13000
Speed	17 knots	18½ knots
Radius	7900 miles	9750 miles
Protection (belt)	18in	12in
Armament	four 13.5in	four 10in
	ten 6in	ten 4.7in

While the *Royal Sovereign*'s and *Centurion*'s were under construction, the new cruisers of the Naval Defence Act were being developed. The *Edgar* first-class vessels were simply smaller versions of the earlier *Blenheim* class of 1888. Six of these were launched between 1891 and 1892 and armed with two single 9.2in guns. They proved to be extremely good sea boats and all exceeded their designed speed on trials, the machinery being extremely reliable. Twenty-eight second-class cruisers were also ordered in the Defence Act and comprised the twenty ships of the *Apollo* class armed with two 6in and six 4.7in, and the eight vessels of the *Astrea* class with two 6in and eight 4.7in. A number of third-class cruisers were also ordered together with thirteen gunboats built to an improved *Rattlesnake* design, and which were completed at the turn of the decade.

During 1891 a new type of 12in gun was under development which was to be mounted in a new vessel specially designed for it. Failing to get the gun into production in time, the Admiralty was forced to redesign the vessel, the *Renown*, and she was completed as a modified *Centurion*. It had been planned that three vessels in the 1892 Estimates should mount the new gun, but the delay in production caused construction of these ships to be postponed for a year. The Controller—Rear-Admiral Fisher—who was also the Third Sea Lord (the post of Controller having been created Third Sea Lord in February 1892) firmly believed in the policy of a battleship carrying the lightest big gun and the largest secondary gun. He wanted at least six more vessels like the *Renown*, but fortunately it was realised that the 10in gun was in fact too light to be of any use, in spite of the fact that the battleship compared favourably with other European warships. With the *Renown* the importance of secondary armament for use against torpedo boat attack went a stage further with the placing of the upper deck guns in casemates. The major feature of the battleship, however, was her protection. For the first time a British warship had the armoured deck sloping down to the lower level of the armour belt. This meant that the waterline armour could be reduced in thickness, thus allowing a greater proportion of protection along the lower deckside.

Not only did this give greater protection, but the armour of the *Renown* was of Harvey steel, a much stronger armour plate than nickel-steel. Harvey armour was an allsteel plate without any welds, and fashioned with a certain amount of carbon on its face, so that when cooled an extremely hard face was produced on the plate. This enabled the belt on the *Renown* to be reduced to 8in on the lower belt and 6in on the upper. The only problem was that Harvey armour could not be used on curved surfaces.

While the *Renown* and *Centurion* were under construction the Admiralty was developing its ideas for means of combating the torpedo boat. Mr. Yarrow, a shipbuilder, engaged in building a number of torpedo boats for foreign powers, was asked by Admiral Fisher if he could build a vessel that would be far superior to a new fast torpedo boat then under construction in a French yard. Mr. Yarrow went to France and saw the new vessels and on his return put forward specifications to the Admiralty for a vessel of 180ft by 18ft developing 4000hp. The basic design was accepted and two vessels were ordered, the *Havock* of 240 tons armed with three 18in torpedo tubes, one 12-pdr and three 6-pdr guns and fitted with a locomotive boiler, and the *Hornet* completed with a new watertube boiler designed by Mr. Yarrow. On trials the *Havock* reached a speed of 26.7 knots on 3500hp while in February 1894 the *Hornet* became the fastest vessel in the world, reaching a speed of 28 knots on trials. As a result of the successful trials 36 vessels known as the "*A*" class or 27 knotters, similar in design to the *Havock*, were ordered under the 1893–1894 Programmes from firms specialising in torpedo boat construction. These early torpedo boat destroyers as they came to be known were often prone to breakdowns, the high speeds maintained when in operation often causing trouble to the hulls where excessive vibration sprung plates and rivets.

The Naval Defence Act was not just a sudden burst of redemption on the part of the Admiralty, but part of a continuous programme of construction that was to ensure Britain's naval supremacy. In future Estimates, three battleships were planned for 1892 and two for 1893. Due to the delays with the 12in gun only the *Renown* was laid down under the 1892 Programme. Lord Charles Beresford remarked upon our apparent naval weaknesses in a public address and asked for Estimates totalling £25m to be spread over a period of 3½ years. He called especially for more cruisers for trade protection. At once support appeared in the form of letters to the press from many naval officers. The Government, however, was very much opposed to any increase in the naval Estimates, looking upon it as their moral duty to reduce military expenditure as much as possible. Then in November 1893 Lord Spencer asked Mr. White to prepare a statement comparing the French and British naval Estimates which were proposed for the next five years. The critical years were at once seen to be 1896–1897, when France and Russia would have built up their navies to such an extent that the Two Power Standard set for the Royal Navy at her present rate of construction would have been almost nullified. The Director of Naval Construction regarded it as imperative that at least six new battleships should be laid down and completed by 1898, this being the absolute minimum which would guarantee the maintenance of the Two Power Standard. Even when presented with the facts, the Government vacillated until the Board of Admiralty threatened to resign in a body. Faced with a mass resignation, the Liberal Government of Gladstone had no alternative but to accept the proposals. Gladstone resigned over the question of the increased expenditure, and was succeeded by Lord Rosebery. As envisaged by Lord Spencer the programme allowed for an expenditure of £31m spread over 5 years (slightly less than that asked for by Lord Beresford) and was designed to see completed 7 *Majestic* class battleships, 2 *Powerful* class cruisers, 6 *Diadem* (first-class cruisers), 12 *Talbot* (second-class cruisers), 4 *Pelorus* (third-class cruisers), 6 ram cruisers, 7 torpedo gunboats, 2 sloops, 82 torpedo boat destroyers (30 knot *B*, *C*, and *D* classes), 30 torpedo boats and one torpedo depot ship.

In spite of Lord Beresford's plea for more cruisers for trade protection, the number planned in the programme was actually reduced, the *Diadem*'s not being ordered until much later and only nine of the *Talbot*'s laid down.

Of the new battleships in the Spencer Programme, the *Majestic* class, the first of which the *Magnificent* was laid down in December 1893, was the largest class of battleships built up to that time. With them White reached the nadir of his career as a designer and from then until he left the Admiralty all his designs were based upon this class. Basically the layout was the same as the *Renown*, but the new 12in, at last ready for service and fitted in the new battleships, was a vast improvement on the earlier weapons. The great advantage of the new gun was its lighter weight compared with the 13.5in gun (SEE TABLE PAGE 13). The weight thus saved was put to use in mounting two extra secondary weapons; a total of twelve 6in and sixteen 12-pdr being carried. In all, nine vessels were built to the *Majestic* design, the last two, *Caesar* and *Illustrious*, differing from the rest in that their turrets were fitted in round barbettes as opposed to the "pear-shaped" ones of the earlier vessels. This design emanated from the *Renown* and was made possible by the all-round loading system. By the use of hydraulic power instead of steam for training the guns the faults of the *Renown* were overcome, and the all-round loading position of the guns gave them a much increased rate of fire in addition to improving the safety of the turret by introducing a break in the ammunition hoist. A change was also made to the charge of the 12in shells. Instead of the gunpowder previously used the new slow-burning cordite was introduced. Cordite gave a far greater pressure in the gun barrel when ignited, and as a result it was possible to make reductions in the size of charges needed (a 12in charge needed 167½lb of cordite as against 295lb of powder). The reduction in the size of the charges meant a large saving in space and weight in the magazines which was used to carry an extra 100 rounds of ammunition for the secondary guns. When completed the *Mars* became the first ship in the Royal Navy to use oil fuel for firing her boilers, and gradually as they became due for refit the rest of the class were so fitted, except the *Jupiter* and *Illustrious*.

In 1893 the navy suffered a disaster to one of its most modern battleships. On June 22 the Mediterranean Fleet was carrying out manoeuvres off the port of Tripoli. The *Victoria*, flagship of the Fleet under the Commander-in-Chief Admiral Sir George Tryon, and the *Camperdown* under Rear-Admiral Hastings Markham were leading the two columns in line ahead six cables apart when Admiral Tryon gave the order for the two columns to turn inwards 16 points in succession. With the large turning circles of the vessels it was inevitable that under these conditions a collision would occur, and it did. The *Camperdown* rammed the *Victoria* on her starboard side just behind the anchor while the vessels were steaming at about 5 knots. Theoretically the *Victoria* should have remained afloat, but many of the watertight doors were not shut in time, and the breach occuring on a transverse bulkhead in the same place as the *Vanguard* had been rammed (SEE VOL. 1 PAGE 59), let the sea enter through the large hole and gather along the starboard side, the flooding being aided by the low freeboard. The *Victoria* rapidly listed to starboard and suddenly capsized and sank, Admiral Tryon and 321 officers and men being drowned. The rest of the squadron managed to avoid similar collisions by dextrously jockeying with their screws.

As the construction of the *Majestic* class proceeded, the cruisers ordered under the Spencer Programme began to be laid down. The two *Powerful* class vessels laid down in 1894, although rated as cruisers were almost as large as the *Majestic*'s (14200 tons as against 14900 tons). They were designed as answers to the Russian *Rurik* and *Rossiya*. The two ships were given a very strong protective deck 6in thick amidships on the slope, but had no armoured belt. For armament they carried a new gun, the 9.2in which was operated electrically and mounted in a barbette protected by 6 inch Harvey armour. Two of these were carried in single mountings fore and aft as well as twelve 6in guns placed in casemates protected by 6 inch armour. These ships were fitted with a new type of boiler first fitted to the torpedo boat destroyer *Hornet* (SEE PAGE 25). The new watertube boiler for the *Powerful* class was built by Belleville and was far superior to the old cylindrical type and materially assisted the *Powerfuls* in maintaining speeds of up to 20 knots throughout their career. The Belleville boilers were very much lighter than cylindrical ones and mechanically were easier to maintain and repair. They were also very economical in their use of fuel, and steam could quickly be raised if the occasion demanded.

Following the *Majestic* class the Admiralty ordered the six vessels of the *Canopus* class. These were to embody all the best features of the *Renown*, *Centurion* and *Majestic*. The main armament was the new 12in gun while the secondary armament, fuel capacity and speed, were to be the same as those in the *Renown*. Finally watertube boilers were to be fitted, and these were the first British battleships to have the new boiler. The Belleville boilers did, however, give rise to certain problems of stability due to their light weight. The sketch designs for the *Canopus* were submitted in May 1895, but before any decision could be reached Lord Rosebery was defeated in a general election and the Conservatives returned to power with Lord Salisbury as Prime Minister and Mr. Goschen as First Lord.

Finally in December 1895 the plans were passed, the first five vessels being laid down under the 1896 Estimates and the *Vengeance* under the 1897 Estimates. In the Autumn of 1896 it was proposed that the vessel should carry twelve 6in guns in casemates instead of the ten planned, those on the main deck being sponsoned to increase end-on fire. The number of 12-pdr was raised from eight to ten and the number of 3-pdr reduced to six as the fighting tops in the masts were to be dispensed with. In addition the *Canopus* class were also the first British warships to carry armour produced by the Krupp process. This had largely superceded the Harvey steel, and its main advantage was that it could be applied to curved surfaces so affording better protection to gun turrets.

Very soon problems began to manifest themselves with the new water-tube boilers. Even after the proving trials in the *Hornet* (SEE PAGE 25) no vessels larger than the torpedo boat destroyer had been fitted with the boiler, and all sorts of difficulties were foreseen, should they be fitted to large warships. The French Belleville watertube boiler was the only one of its type advanced enough to be fitted in the *Powerful* and *Canopus* classes. In spite of its many advantages it did not prove fully satisfactory owing to its inexpert operation by officers untrained in handling the delicate machinery. Of course, as had happened before with other new inventions, there were many in the Admiralty and the navy who were opposed to change, and they at once opened a vigorous campaign against the intro-duction of the new boiler. They were supported by a number of in-dustrialists who had invested their money in the development of cylindrical boilers. The main fault of the watertube boiler, however, lay in the fact that it was rushed into service before engineers could be trained in its operation, or firms experienced enough in its construction.

Finally the outbursts against the watertube boiler became so vociferous that a Committee of Inquiry was appointed to investigate the claims for and against the boiler. The first move of the Committee was to recommend that for the time being no more Belleville boilers be fitted to HM ships until it had been thoroughly tested. In the meantime a ridiculous state of affairs existed with vessels being completed with mixtures of cylindrical and watertube boilers. Instead of the Belleville a number of other makes were tried in the navy, amongst these being the Niclausse, Babcock and Wilcox and the Yarrow. After a number of tests the Niclausse was abandoned altogether, having none of the advantages of the Belleville and many of its alleged disadvantages. Instead the Admiralty decided to fit the Babcock and Wilcox and the Yarrow large tube type boilers. Gradually fears about the watertube boilers abated as the problems were ironed out, and the Admiralty proceeded to adopt the Belleville as its main watertube boiler for all new battleships.

The expansion of the German Empire in East Africa created grave misgivings in neighbouring African States, especially in the island of Zanzibar. Relations with Britain deteriorated as the mainland possessions of the Sultan were taken over by the Germans, with of course British agreement. In 1896 the Sultan died, and Prince Seyyid Khalid ben Barghash mounted a revolution with the full support of the army. He stormed the Royal Palace broke out his personal flag and proclaimed himself as the new Sultan. The cruiser *Philomel* and the gunboat *Thrush* happened to be in the harbour at the time and at once landed all available men. Later another gunboat arrived, and the *Thrush* was then moved across the harbour to where her guns could bear on the Palace. The following day the cruisers *St. George*, with Rear-Admiral Sir Harry Rawson on board, and *Racoon* arrived and the three other warships moored in a line with all their guns trained on the Palace. At 0700 on August 28, 1896, the rebel Prince was given a final ultimatum to surrender. As the British vessels prepared for action all foreign vessels left the harbour, leaving the *Glasgow*, the late Sultan's gunboat now manned by the rebels. Two hours later when the ultimatum expired the British opened fire, the bombardment lasting just over half an hour, during which time the Palace was destroyed, the *Glasgow* severely damaged and several dhows sunk. At this Prince Seyyid Khalid ben Barghash surrendered, and a new Sultan was proclaimed.

With the French and Japanese completing their superior battleships *Jena* and *Shikishima* it was decided under the 1897 Programme to order a larger and more powerful British battleship. As a result three vessels known as the *Formidable* class were ordered. A newer and heavier mark of 12in gun was mounted that developed a far higher muzzle velocity and energy than earlier marks, and was fitted into a new mounting which allowed rapid loading in any position of elevation or training. The new gun, however, needed a much heavier turntable and mounting and a much larger barbette which took up most of the weight saved by fitting lighter boilers and thinner Krupp armour. In the completed design White planned to keep to the displacement of the earlier *Majestic* design while at the same time introducing all the improvements evolved since that ship was completed. He also hoped to increase the secondary armament to fourteen guns. The Admiralty, however, only requested twelve 6in guns, but asked that the protection on the citadel be increased to 9in. With all the modifications and ensuing extra weight the final displacement of the

Formidable class only exceeded that of the *Majestic* by 100 tons. They were far superior vessels, being easier to handle, and answering well to the helm.

In addition to the *Formidable* class six armoured cruisers of the *Cressy* class were ordered in the 1897–1898 Estimates. These vessels were very similar to the *Powerful* class, but slightly smaller with an identical armament of 9.2in and 6in as opposed to just the 6in of their predecessors, the *Diadem* class. The *Cressy* class differed in having an armoured belt 6in thick. The *Cressy*'s were followed by a class of four armoured cruisers in which the design faults of earlier vessels were eradicated. Displacement was increased by 2000 tons, allowing the class to mount four extra 6in casemate guns. The calibre of the main armament was also raised from the 40 of the *Cressy* class to 45. All in all the *Drake* class cruisers proved far superior to the *Cressy* class. The *Drake*'s were followed by ten armoured cruisers of the *County* class. Lord Beresford's pleas for more fast cruisers to protect trade routes had at long last been heeded by the Admiralty. Many cruisers were now under construction in all categories of this type of warship. The *County* class armoured cruisers were much smaller than the *Drake*'s and in place of the 9.2in guns carried 6in guns in electrically controlled twin turrets fore and aft. The vessels of the *County* class had originally been intended to have 7.5in, but these were discarded in favour of the twin 6in, which however, proved somewhat of a failure, the turrets working space being exceedingly cramped greatly reducing the efficiency of the weapon. As a whole the class was no more than rather better versions of the earlier *Talbot*'s. As armoured cruisers the *County* class were far too lightly protected and the guns were not nearly large enough. The 7.5in originally planned for the vessels would have been ideal, but even then they would have had insufficient protection. Had they been rated as first or second-class protected cruisers they would have been ideal.

At the beginning of 1897 the Royal Navy was again called into action yet again on the West coast of Africa. The tribes of the Benin region were posing a threat to the Niger Coast Protectorate, and to eliminate this threat a squadron of six cruisers and three gunboats under command of Rear-Admiral Sir Harry Rawson was sent to calm the area. With Hausa troops to make up the numbers, Admiral Rawson landed a force of 1200 men on February 9, 1897, and began a march on Benin through the fever ridden bush. After fighting tribesmen most of the way the force finally reached the city of Benin on February 18. Admiral Rawson garrisoned the abandoned city with Hausa troops and returned to the coast leaving the politicians in Lagos to conclude a treaty with the Benin chiefs.

While Admiral Rawson was sorting out the problems in West Africa, the British Army had been advancing in the Sudan, at last forcing the Mahdi's Dervishes on the run. The Mahdi himself had died in 1886, but the Dervishes were still a force to be reckoned with under the leadership of the Khalifa. To supply the army as it moved south into the wastes of the Sudan a railway was constructed, the line following closely the course of the Nile, where river gunboats could protect the supply trains. In charge of the army was Herbert Kitchener, and the navy seconded men to operate the gunboats under Kitchener's orders. In charge of the naval force was Commander Colville of the battleship *Nile*, assisted by Lieutenants David Beatty, Walter Cowan, and Horace Hood. The force consisted of four shallow draught stern-wheel gunboats normally stationed on the Nile and armed with maxim guns. In addition three modern gunboats were shipped out to Egypt in sections and assembled on the Nile. The gunboats followed hard upon the heels of the army, negotiating the treacherous cataracts of the Nile with the help of bands of natives who acted as human tugs towing the boats over the most difficult passages. After a number of brushes with the Dervishes, the army and the gunboats finally reached Omdurman where after a close action the Dervishes were completely routed, 10883 of a total force of 80000 being killed in precipitate charges against the army, and fire from the gunboats.

This, however, was not the end of the enterprise, for a few days later Kitchener received intelligence that a French force had arrived at Fashoda. Again use was made of the gunboats, which took Kitchener and a party of troops up the Nile to investigate. On arrival the British found that the French had laid claim to the Sudan as liberators of the territory. The French force was only a small one, and with the imposing strength of the river gunboats, Kitchener had no difficulty in persuading the French commander to recognise British sovereignty over the area.

The Hon. Charles Parsons made history in 1894 when he ran the trials of a new vessel which he had designed. It was not so much the vessel herself that was unique, but her method of propulsion. Parsons had developed an idea whose principle had been known for centuries. Turning theory into practise Parsons fitted the new ship with turbines that he had constructed, naming the vessel *Turbinia*. With a compound radial flow turbine driving a single shaft, the $44\frac{1}{2}$-ton vessel at once ran into trouble, the speed developed being only $19\frac{3}{4}$ knots. Deciding that the slow speed was being caused by cavities around the propeller blades, Parsons re-engined the vessel with three turbines driving three shafts, each of which had three screws. Success was achieved, *Turbinia* reaching a speed of

29.6 knots. It was decided to change the propellers, when an even better result was obtained, the speed exceeding 32 knots.

Admiral Fisher inspected *Turbinia* in February 1897 and the following June she was present at the Jubilee Review where she showed her capabilities by reaching a speed of 30 knots in 40 seconds. With this success Parsons put forward a suggestion to the Admiralty that they should build a 30 knot type of torpedo boat destroyer powered by turbines. The Board of Admiralty accepted Parsons tender in 1898 and the torpedo boat destroyer, now named destroyer for short, was laid down. The following year the Admiralty purchased a turbine powered vessel from the firm of Elswick, renaming her *Cobra*. Both vessels reached well over 30 knots on their trials, a vindication of the faith Parsons had put in his turbines.

June 1897 was the Diamond Jubilee of Queen Victoria. To mark the event the Royal Navy staged the largest and most impressive array of warships ever seen in the world. In all 165 ships were assembled at Spithead, including 22 battleships, 40 cruisers and 20 torpedo boats all drawn from home waters. This was a truly staggering comment on the strength of the Royal Navy, except that a number of the vessels in the review were unfortunately incapable of steaming and had to be towed to their positions. The Germans, however, were not to know this, neither did they look upon the assembly as just a Jubilee Review. The Queen herself did not attend, not being very enamoured with the Royal Yacht *Victoria and Albert*, she commanded the Prince of Wales to review the fleet. To Admiral Tirpitz this was a frightening eye opener, as every one of the vessels at Spithead came from bases around Britain. Not one vessel came from a foreign station. With such a display of strength Tirpitz at once set about goading the German nation into action, and the following year, 1898, the First German Navy Law was passed. The arms race was on.

CHAPTER 3

Gunnery and Reforms

*It would have been as though he were in a boat of stone
with masts of steel, sails of lead, ropes of iron, the devil
at the helm, the wrath of God for a breeze, and hell for
his destination*

EMORY A. STORRS, 1866

THE YEAR 1900 found the Royal Navy yet again on active service, this time in the Far East. European incursion into Chinese affairs and trading interests in the country had aroused the feelings of a large section of the community in Northern China. The Dowager Empress, Tzu Hsi, was also contemptuous of the foreigners in her land, and with her connivance, bands of fanatical Chinese, known popularly as Boxers, proceeded to harass Christian communities and foreign sympathisers. The incidents spread until at last, at the request of the British legation in Peking, Admiral Seymour sent guards to protect the settlement. This was not sufficient and in June 1900 Admiral Seymour took a force to the mouth of the Peiho River where a landing party composed of British and Foreign troops and a number of sailors was put ashore. The party tried to force its way up country to Peking, but this only aroused the Boxers, who then laid seige to the Foreign legations in Peking. Admiral Seymour's force was held up for about a month at Tientsin, but after being heavily reinforced managed to force a way through to the capital, which was taken in August 1900. As a final show of force the city was systematically sacked. Among the outstanding naval officers taking part in the action was Commander Beatty of the *Barfleur*, who was promoted to Captain for his part in the fighting around Tientsin.

Under the 1898–1900 Programmes eleven more battleships were ordered. Five of these belonged to the *London* class, which were virtually repeats of the *Formidable*'s. The other six vessels, the *Duncan* class, were a new design. The Admiralty laid down the specifications for the class after obtaining details of the Russian *Osliabia* and *Peresviet*. The *Duncan*'s were

34

slightly smaller than the *Formidable*'s and lacked ventilators, a feature which distinguished them from previous battleships. When completed they were far superior to the Russian vessels, but in order to obtain a higher speed they had sacrificed some of their protection. By reducing the amidships belt from 9in to 7in a saving of 1000 tons was made on the displacement, while the horsepower was increased by 3000. In spite of all this the speed of the vessels was only raised by one knot over that of the *London* class.

By 1900 the submarine had become a weapon in its own right, adopted by the American, French, Russian and Turkish navies. At last the Admiralty decided that submarines should form a branch of the Royal Navy, and so in the 1900–1901 Programme, after carefully studying all the types then in use abroad, five *Holland* type American boats were ordered from Vickers at Barrow. The hull was of cigar shape and propulsion on the surface was provided by a single petrol engine, with electric motors for submerged power. These first submarines of the Royal Navy were used for evaluation, training and instructional purposes, rather than for any warlike uses. A number of officers still regarded submarines with suspicion and it was some time before the submarine arm of the navy was fully accepted.

As soon as the *Holland*'s were in service a class of fourteen new vessels, the "*A*" class was ordered from Vickers. From this time development of the submarine proceeded rapidly under the guidance of James McKechnie. Working with him on submarine development was T. G. Owens Thurston, who carried out many experiments at the Vickers experimental tank at St. Albans. Short periscopes and high conning towers were characteristic features of these early submarines. *A 13* was experimentally fitted with a heavy diesel oil engine which was a vast improvement on the petrol engine, and was subsequently fitted to all new submarines. The fuel oil of the diesel engine had a much higher flash point than petrol and much reduced the danger of the fuel supply igniting from stray sparks.

The "*A*" class were followed by eleven vessels of the "*B*" class, *B 1* actually being *A 14* renumbered. Following the tragic loss of *A 1* in March 1904 (she was accidentally rammed by the liner *Berwick Castle*) all the "*B*" class were fitted with two periscopes, one for navigation and the other for search purposes.

For years the main criticism of the navy's warships had been that they were undergunned, the main blame for which fell on the Director of Naval Construction. In fact White was only responsible for designing the vessels, the specifications being laid down by the Board of Admiralty. It was their policy never to initiate improvements or changes which might force foreign powers to develop vessels which could nullify our numerical superiority, instead they waited for foreign developments, and improved upon them.

As soon as details of the latest American and Italian battleships became known, the Controller, Sir Arthur Wilson, ordered a series of new designs to be prepared which would allow for a heavier secondary armament. As the Admiralty did not lay down any specifications for the new vessels it was left to the Director of Naval Construction to make suggestions and draw up plans. White was away ill at the time and the task fell to the Chief Constructor Mr. Deadman and his assistant J. H. Narbeth. The Admiralty did not accept the design prepared by Mr. Deadman whereupon Mr. Narbeth designed a vessel based upon the *Duncan*, but having an intermediate armament of either 9.2in or 7.5in. The Admiralty approved a design which mounted eight 7.5in guns on the upper deck in pairs, and a secondary battery of 6in sited on the main deck. Before the design was completed White returned to office, and the Board of Admiralty asked him to prepare a report. White asked Narbeth if there were any improvements he would like to make to his design, and an alternative plan with a single 9.2in gun in place of the paired 7.5in was proposed. White, who concurred with his assistant's proposals, then requested the Admiralty to accept the new plans. The change from 7.5in to 9.2in had so little effect on the general design and displacement that the plans were redrawn and completed in a very short time.

Finally the ill health that had dogged White for so long forced him to leave the Admiralty and in 1902 he was succeeded by Philip Watts from Elswick. Watts also approved of the new design and signed the plans for the new battleship that was to be called the *King Edward VII*. A total of eight vessels of the new class were ordered under the 1901–02–03 Estimates. When they entered service there was some criticism of the mixed main armament of 12in and 9.2in, which created many problems with fire control. There were many who felt that it would have been better to mount six 9.2in in pairs instead of the two single 9.2in and five single 6in guns. The 9.2in at the time was an excellent weapon, being as easy to handle as the 6in and almost as quick to fire. The 6in battery on the main deck was also severely criticised, the main point being that it was only $12\frac{3}{4}$ feet above the waterline and in a heavy sea it would be extremely difficult to operate the guns, as they would be continuously swept by the sea. Not only that but if the vessels rolled to 14 degrees the barrels of the guns would dip into the sea. Consequently a number of the vessels later had these guns removed. Protection was similar to that of the *London* class, but was rendered obsolete during their construction when the capped shell was introduced, which had a much higher velocity and increased powers of penetration. The class also suffered from the "boiler dispute" (SEE PAGE 29) and only the *Commonwealth* and *Dominion* had all watertube boilers, the rest of the class having a mixture of cylindrical and watertube.

The loss of the torpedo boat destroyer *Cobra* in 1901 during a gale led to a close inspection on the methods of construction of the destroyer. In the 1902 Programme a new class of destroyer, the *River*'s, was ordered, with a high forecastle deck instead of the turtle-back construction of the earlier vessels. It was also realised that the speed of 30 knots at light load requested for the earlier vessels was unrealistic, especially in heavy seas, and this was reduced to 25 knots in the new class, which speed was to be attained under service conditions and normal load. It was decided also to fit the class with reciprocating machinery, in spite of the problems encountered in the preceding classes. Only the *Eden* of the new class was fitted with a Parsons turbine.

At the turn of the decade the outbreak of the South African War (Boer War) and Great Britain's feelings towards German support for the Boers, forced the German Secretary of State for Naval Affairs, Admiral Tirpitz, to draw up plans for a much larger navy. Under the 1900 Germany Navy Law not only was the Fleet to be greatly expanded but two battle squadrons were to be kept fully manned ready for action while another two squadrons would form a reserve fleet, of which half would be kept in permanent commission.

These plans at once placed the British Navy in jeopardy. Being built on a Two Power Standard (SEE PAGE 20) with the two potential enemies looked upon as France and Russia, the Royal Navy could not hope, in the state it was in at the time, to compete with the German Navy as well. Britain no longer able to isolate herself from continental involvement was forced to look for an alliance. As a result a treaty was signed with Japan in 1901 and attempts at reconciliation with France and Russia were begun. These efforts finally bore fruit when the *Entente Cordiale* came into being in 1904. At the same time Germany, in spite of her increasingly antagonistic outlook towards Great Britain, was invited to join the Alliance with Japan.

In June 1902 Captain Fisher was appointed Second Sea Lord with responsibility for the manning and training of the Fleet in preparation for war, a post he held until the following August when he was made Commander-in-Chief of Portsmouth. For Captain Fisher this was an extremely important post, and during this period of command he crystallised his idea on battleship design, which finally led to the ordering of the *Dreadnought* and high speed battlecruiser. Apart from theoretical matters Admiral Fisher also busied himself with practical plans. For many years the higher education of officers in the Royal Navy had been a disgrace. This was not all, for the methods and subjects taught were old fashioned and any independant thought or action was always discouraged. Admiral Fisher was well aware of this sad state of affairs and one of the first tasks he set himself on becoming Commander of Portsmouth was to set about improving the educational standard of the navy. As a start he put forward proposals for the establishment of two naval colleges, at Osborne on the Isle of Wight, and at Dartmouth.

In 1903 two battleships laid down for Chile were purchased by the Royal Navy to prevent any other European power acquiring them. Renamed *Swiftsure* and *Triumph* the two vessels did not match any of our own fleet, being designed by Edward Reed to Chilean requirements. They were long and narrow to enable them to dock in Chile, and the main armament was comprised of four 10in guns, a calibre not in use in the Royal Navy. In spite of the fact that the vessels only carried 10in guns, they were so sited that the vessels could deliver a broadside equal to that of any other vessel then afloat, each gun being capable of firing eight rounds a minute. They also carried the heaviest anti-torpedo armament of any British battleship, in the form of fourteen 14-pdr.

For some years Captain Percy Scott had complained of the gunnery of the Royal Navy. Being an expert in the field he was appointed to the command of the gunnery school at Whale Island in 1903, where he at once set about putting into practice all the theories he had worked out. The old methods of instruction from a book were discarded and henceforth gunnery efficiency was achieved by practical methods. Many of the Battle Practises held by the Fleet in which long range gunnery was carried out were useless as the vessels were not provided with the necessary instruments or instructions. The problem was how to register hits when the target could not be exploded or made to catch fire.

To try out some of his theories Scott asked the Admiralty if he could use the armoured cruiser *Drake*, commanded by Captain J. R. Jellicoe, as a target. To spot the fall of shot accurately Scott believed that broadside firing was essential, and for this purpose he intended to have the *Drake* straddled with broadsides. The Admiralty refused to allow Scott to use the *Drake* for such a purpose, instead instructing Rear-Admiral Sir Reginald Custance and Rear-Admiral Sir Hedworth Lambton of the *Venerable* and *Victorious* to experiment with long range firing. To assist them carry out their experiments no restrictions were placed on the amount of ammunition to be used. Scott had also made many complaints to the Admiralty about the poor sights used on the guns. This also took some years to improve, and not until 1905, when director fire was first instituted, did gunnery really begin to improve.

The *Cressy* class armoured cruisers of 1899–1901 were followed by the *Drake, Kent,* and *Devonshire* class armoured cruisers, and were built in reply to the French armoured cruisers. As such, they were to be responsible for protecting the trade routes, replacing the older and less powerful cruisers. Philip Watts' conception of the armoured cruiser was different from White's, as he believed that armoured cruisers should be faster and more heavily armed and protected so that they could work with the Battle Fleet and act as scouts, keeping watch on the German *Kaiser, Wittelsbach* and *Brauenschweig* type battleships. Watts' ideal was a vessel mounting plenty of heavy guns, preferably the 9.2in, which in his opinion was an excellent weapon. With such views the *Duke of Edinburgh* class armoured cruisers were designed, armed with a single 9.2in fore and aft, and two on either beam fore and aft. They were designed to make 23 knots under service conditions, but this meant that they would not be able to have the protection of a battleship, or carry such a heavy broadside. A broadside of 6in guns was, however, felt to be perfectly adequate. Although on paper the ideas behind the *Duke of Edinburgh* class appeared sound, in practice they were a failure. To begin with the 6in battery was found to be mounted too low, the guns being unworkable in anything except a very calm sea. Thus in the mock battle manoeuvres of 1906 the *Black Prince,* continually washed by heavy seas, was soon put out of action by the *Leviathan.* In addition to this the anti-torpedo armament was totally inadequate. A total of twenty 3-pdr were carried, and were well sited, but far too small a weapon to be of any use against a torpedo boat destroyer. The *Duke of Edinburgh* class was followed by four similar vessels of the *Warrior* class, laid down in 1904. They were to have been of the same type as the *Duke of Edinburgh,* but with the 6in secondary armament proving inadequate, they were redesigned to mount 7.5in guns on the upper deck in turrets. With gunnery becoming more scientific and complicated these vessels were fitted with fire control platforms in the masts from which the guns were directed. Thus armed these vessels proved formidable opponents. They were excellent sea boats, so steady that the guns could be worked in practically any kind of weather.

The *Minotaur* class followed, being laid down in 1905. They carried only four 9.2in in twin turrets, but an extra six 7.5in. It was at last realised that the 3-pdr gun was too small to be any good as an anti-torpedo weapon and so the *Minotaur* class carried sixteen 12-pdr. Difficulties over the watertube boiler had at last been resolved and this class carried a full set of the new boilers.

As the *Swiftsure* and *Triumph* had been purchased in 1903, the Admiralty decided that only two battleships were needed for the 1904 Estimates instead of the three originally planned. Watts put forward plans for a vessel mounting twelve 9.2in in twin turrets amidships and four 12in in twin turrets fore and aft. The plans were passed by the Controller, Sir William May, but the Board of Admiralty did not approve. The main obstacle was the beam necessary to carry the 9.2in guns. The vessels had to be accommodated in the docks at Chatham or Devonport, and these were not wide enough to take the vessels as designed by Watts. Consequently they were redesigned to carry ten 9.2in in four twin and two single turrets amidships. After making a close study of the relationships between gun power and protection in earlier vessels, the Controller found that better protection was needed over a larger area of the vessel than had been hitherto obtained. As a result, the protection of the *Lord Nelson* class as the new vessels were known, was improved, the vessels being given solid bulkheads. To save weight necessary for the extra protection it was decided to dispense with the secondary armament. It was felt that in any case secondary armament was of little value as it would be put out of use long before the range had decreased sufficiently for it to be brought into action. The vessels were delayed somewhat during construction as their main armament was appropriated for the *Dreadnought* then under construction.

In October 1904, Admiral Fisher became First Sea Lord, a post which gave him the opportunity to initiate many of the reforms and much of the reorganisation which had held his attention for so many years. Upon taking office he at once set about defining the duties of the Board of Admiralty (SEE APPENDIX 1). For many years the Board had carried on its affairs in what almost amounted to confusion, the different problems and day to day matters being dealt with by whoever happened to be at hand. After having set the Board of Admiralty on a clear course, Admiral Fisher began his great programme of reform and organisation, some details of which he had already set in motion during his period as Commander of Portsmouth (SEE PAGE 38).

Admiral Fisher's first main concern was to get an efficient fighting fleet, and as a step towards this he set up a great economy drive, cutting out much wastage and duplication. To curb unnecessary expenditure the First

Sea Lord set up the Navy Estimates Committee. During the first four years of the decade the Estimates had nearly trebled and these were carefully scrutinised by the Committee to find ways of reducing the rising expenditure. For instance the medical department ordered one set of glass water tumblers and the supply department another!

The next area in which economies could be made was in the warships themselves. The Admiralty had always been loth to scrap old vessels, and many antiquated ships, better suited as museum pieces, were kept on the lists entailing the expenditure of vast sums of money on their maintenance and repairs. Admiral Fisher scrapped them all, including many of the protected cruisers, which under modern conditions had been made obsolete by the existence of armoured cruisers. In all a total of 154 vessels were removed from the Fleet, and even then this was not quite as many as Fisher had asked to be scrapped. The dockyards were also reorganised and 6000 men sacked, while the overseas dockyards were heavily reduced in size.

The new Selborne education scheme, begun while Fisher was in command at Portsmouth, was also enlarged. The two new colleges at Osborne and Dartmouth opened the way for a common entry for men in all classes of society to have equal chances of becoming officers, with part of their fees paid by the state. Not only that, but the initial training of all officer branches in the Royal Navy was amalgamated into the two colleges, instead of each branch being trained separately as previously. On reaching the rank of Lieutenant, at about 22 years of age, the officers at last began to specialise in either the gunnery, torpedo, navigation, engineer or general officer branches. At the start the Royal Marines had also been combined in the scheme but this was soon found to be impracticable, and the Marines continued to have a separate training from other naval officers.

Simultaneously with the improvements in education Fisher also brought up to date the promotion boards and conditions of service. There had been an age limit at which officers could reach flag rank, and this led to many older Admirals being given commands which they could not really manage. The First Sea Lord believed that with a modern navy younger officers with new ideas were needed and to obtain these men, the age limit was lowered by approximately four years. At the same time it was decided to pension off officers two or three years earlier if there were no suitable posts for them. With these changes in force the average age of officers was considerably lowered, Captains gaining their rank at about 36 years, Rear-Admirals at 41 and Vice-Admirals at 52 years of age.

Conditions on the lower deck were still poor when Admiral Fisher went to the Admiralty. This concerned him greatly and he realised that unless the men were happy and contented the fighting efficiency of the Fleet would not be at its best. For example the quantity of food allocated to each man every day was increased, and to give the men the opportunity of having fresh bread each day bakeries were fitted in all the larger warships. Cutlery was also provided for the seamen's mess-decks. Living quarters were also improved, with better ventilation and heating, and the sanitation was modernised.

In order that all the valuable training a man was given should not be lost, the First Sea Lord formed the Royal Fleet Reserve. On leaving the navy ratings were encouraged to join the Royal Fleet Reserve, which to some extent reduced the importance of the Royal Naval Reserve, which was composed of merchant seamen. The training of the Royal Naval Reserve was improved, the men being sent to sea in commissioned ships, the old sailing vessels previously used as training hulks being scrapped. In 1903 a further Reserve had been formed called the Royal Naval Volunteer Reserve. This reserve was created from volunteers drawn from yachtsmen and fishermen who were prepared to give up their own jobs in time of war and serve in the navy.

The War Course begun in 1900 was also extended in scope and purpose. Admiral Fisher had also initiated this. It was a compulsory course lasting eight months for officers of Commander and Captains rank. Its aims were to study the methods of conducting war and the investigation of different tactical problems. After a few courses had been held it was found that eight months was too long a period over which to conduct the lectures. In 1903 the prospectus was altered slightly and two courses were held every year lasting four months. The syllabus ranged over a wide area of naval affairs, including naval history, strategy, tactics and international law.

In 1890 and 1900 German Navy Laws posed a serious threat to the Royal Navy's mastery of the seas. To counter this threat Admiral Fisher began to reorganise the composition of the fleets. The problem was most serious in home waters where for the larger part of the year the Channel Fleet (renamed from the Channel Squadron in 1903) was on exercise in Irish and Spanish waters. While it was away there were no organised squadrons available to deal with any difficult situations. The only vessels available were antiquated battleships of the Reserve Squadron, which was retitled Home Fleet in 1903. This force was practically useless, the vessels being deployed about in harbours all round the coasts of Britain, and manned by only two thirds of their complement. Even if fully manned, the squadron was incapable of meeting an organised force as it only exercised for about a fortnight every year, the ships being left at anchor for the rest of the time. In an even worse state were the ships of the Fleet Reserve and Dockyard Reserve. These vessels were almost completely closed down, having just care and maintenance parties on board the Fleet Reserve vessels, and only watchmen on the Dockyard Reserve vessels.

As a start to building up the strength in Home waters, Fisher introduced the nucleus crew system, whereby those vessels in the Fleet Reserve, later renamed Reserve Fleet, were crewed with all the officers and specialists necessary for the fighting efficiency of the vessel, giving them two-fifths of their normal complement. These vessels were then concentrated in the dockyards of Devonport, Portsmouth and Sheerness. In addition to this the ships were regularly taken to sea for fortnightly training cruises, and their complements were brought up to full strength for the annual manoeuvres in which the vessels participated. The extra men needed to man these vessels were taken from the ships which Fisher had scrapped.

Apart from improving the state of the Reserve Fleets Admiral Fisher also completely reorganised the Active Fleets. In view of the international situation (the Alliance with Japan, friendlier relations with France, and the forming of the *Entente Cordiale* and rising German naval power) the major part of the navy was held in home waters. The number of active squadrons was reduced from nine to five, based on Alexandria, Dover, Gibraltar, Singapore and Simonstown. From 1904 two Fleets were kept in home waters, these being the Home Fleet, based at Dover, and the Atlantic Fleet, based at Gibraltar. To increase the strengths of these fleets a number of battleships were brought home from the Far East and the Mediterranean. Being based at Gibraltar, the Atlantic Fleet was in an ideal position to reinforce either the Mediterranean or Home Fleet. In addition to this strengthening of the navy, the new armoured cruisers as they were completed, were formed into squadrons and attached to the Home and Atlantic Fleets.

CHAPTER 4

The Dreadnought and Admiral Fisher

He who has possession of the Sea must of necessity be
master of the situation

CICERO

THE CONCEPTION of the dreadnought type of warship is attributed to Constructor General Cuniberti of the Italian Navy, who set forth his ideas in the 1903 edition of Fred T. Jane's annual "Fighting Ships". General Cuniberti pointed out that there were two ways of dealing with an enemy—either by a knockout blow or a slow process of attrition. This would result from two totally different types of action. The destruction of an enemy by attrition was the method practised by the Royal Navy in 1905, and was necessitated because most of the warships then in service throughout the world were of comparative fighting powers. The other method, the knockout blow, would require a type of vessel which the Royal Navy did not at that time possess. Its armour would have to be impervious to all known weapons and its own armament must be heavy enough to penetrate an enemy's armour at his most vulnerable point, the waterline belt. To achieve this the speed of the vessel must be higher than any other known vessel. With six such vessels General Cuniberti felt the Royal Navy could easily retain the mastery of the seas. The specifications for such a vessel were a displacement of 17000 tons, dimensions of 521 × 82 × 27ft with a 12in armour belt along the waterline and round the battery, twelve 12in guns with ample ammunition and anti-torpedo weapons, and a speed of 24 knots.

At first these plans were ridiculed in Great Britain as being technically unpractical and unrealistic as they would render our present fleet of capital ships obsolete. Following the Russo-Japanese War in 1904–1905, the Japanese laid down the *Aki* and *Satsuma*, whose conception followed along the lines of General Cuniberti's ideas. The American's also took note of these ideas and ordered the two battleships *Michigan* and *South Carolina*.

44

In Britain Admiral Fisher had been turning over similar ideas in his mind since his time as Commander-in-Chief of Portsmouth. Finally in October 1904 he put forward proposals for a British battleship to be constructed along similar lines. The design was for a vessel carrying ten 12in guns in five turrets so sited that eight guns could bear on the broadside and six ahead or astern. (This was an adaption of the *Lord Nelson* disposition.) The grouping of eight guns on a broadside was chosen as it was found to be the most efficient unit for fire control when firing salvoes for ranging. Eight guns was also the maximum number that could probably be fired simultaneously with full charges without causing serious strain to the vessel. The designed speed of the new vessel was 21 knots, three knots less than the speed suggested by General Cuniberti.

The advances in warship design over the last few decades, and more particularly the improvements made in the field of gunnery more or less made the evolution of the dreadnought type warships inevitable. This was in the main due to the greater ranges at which gunnery was now practised, and also to the possibility of long range torpedo attacks. Greatly increased gun ranges were possible mainly as a result of the efforts of Admiral Percy Scott who practised the art of salvo firing to aid in spotting the fall of shot and ranging. This was only really feasible when heavy armament of a uniform calibre was mounted.

At the same time Admiral Fisher put forward ideas for another vessel of similar design but different conception. This ship was a high speed version of the previous vessel with protection sacrificed to gain a speed of 25 knots so as to bring it more in line with General Cuniberti's ideal. This new design became known as the battlecruiser.

The design for the new battleship was finalised in March 1905 and the vessel was laid down in October 1905 as the *Dreadnought*. Although foreign dreadnought type vessels were being planned at that time, Great Britain led the world in dreadnought design, completing the *Dreadnought* in the incredibly short time of a year for so large and complex a vessel.

The *Dreadnought* was extremely well protected, the hull generally being immensely strong and the scantlings very heavy. The armour itself was disposed as in the *Lord Nelson*, except that a certain amount was applied internally below the waterline for protection against the possibility of the detonation of two torpedoes in any position. The *Dreadnought* also had solid bulkheads. Apart from armament the new vessel was also unique in that she was powered by turbines. Previously these had only been fitted to destroyers and small cruisers. The plans to equip the *Dreadnought* with turbines gave rise to much apprehension, especially when the three other vessels ordered under the 1906 Programme were also given turbines. It was the fitting of the turbines which gave the *Dreadnought* her high speed of 21 knots, three knots more than the *Lord Nelson*.

In some respects the *Dreadnought* did not quite come up to the specifications suggested by General Cuniberti, and neither did the battlecruiser.

TABLE 3

	Displacement	Speed	Armament	Protection (Belt)
Cuniberti design	17000 tons	24 knots	12-12in, 18-12pdr	12in
Dreadnought	17800 tons	21 knots	10-12in, 27-12pdr	11in
Invincible	17250 tons	25 knots	8-12in, 16-4in	6in

In the battlecruisers—the *Invincible*, *Inflexible* and *Indomitable*, armour was sacrificed in order that the speed suggested by General Cuniberti could be achieved. Unlike the beam turret disposition in the *Dreadnought*, those in the battlecruiser were sited *en enchelon*. By such a siting it was planned that the battlecruisers would obtain the same broadside as the *Dreadnought*, while mounting only four turrets. In practise, however, it was found that only six guns could bear on either beam instead of the eight planned. The battlecruisers were completed two years after the *Dreadnought*, by which time the Admiralty had realised that some sort of secondary armament was essential to a large warship, and so it was decided to arm them with the new 4in QF that had just been designed. The main purpose behind the design of these vessels was to scout for and engage the enemy at long range, keeping him occupied until the main fleet of dreadnoughts arrived.

Just before the end of its term of office at the end of 1905, the Conservative Government laid down the shipbuilding policy to be followed for the navy by the next Government, irrespective of who was returned to power. Known as the Cawdor Programme, after the Conservative's First Lord of the Admiralty, it specified that four armoured ships of the dreadnought and battlecruiser type be ordered each year, thus ensuring that at any time eight such vessels would be under construction.

The party returned to power at the General Election was the Liberal Party under Sir Henry Campbell Bannerman. Although not in favour of heavy expenditure on armaments they accepted the principles set out in the Cawdor Programme. This programme planned that the Royal Navy should have in commission in 1908, five dreadnoughts and three battlecruisers as opposed to Germany's two dreadnoughts.

The 1906–1907 Estimates provided for the construction of one dread-nought and three battlecruisers. At first the Liberal Party accepted these figures, but after having passed the Estimates the Government had a change of mind, and in an effort to reduce arms expenditure so that it could carry out its programme of social reform, the Estimates were reduced to three improved *Dreadnought* type vessels. The three vessels finally ordered were the *Bellerophon*, *Superb* and *Temeraire*. They were almost identical to the *Dreadnought* but of slightly greater displacement.

In October 1906 Admiral Fisher set about reorganising the Fleets. This at once led to dissension in the ranks and Lord Beresford was highly critical of Admiral Fisher's decisions. With the nucleus crew system (SEE PAGE 43) now well established Admiral Fisher felt able to carry out far reaching reforms among the warships stationed around Great Britain. Until 1906 there had been three independant battleship divisions stationed around our coasts, but in that year these divisions—the Nore, Portsmouth and Devonport, were combined into one fleet—the Home Fleet. This fleet, under the command of one Commander-in-Chief, became the main force when the Channel Fleet was away on exercises. To bring the new Home Fleet up to a strength capable of meeting any threat, two battleships were withdrawn from each of the Channel, Atlantic and Mediterranean Fleets. The remaining seven vessels of the Home Fleet were drawn from the former Fleet Reserve.

These moves led to a great public outcry, but Admiral Fisher was not to be put off from his reorganisation, which continued throughout his term of office. Gradually the Home Fleet was built up until finally the Nore Division on its own was powerful enough to meet any threat posed by the German Navy.

In spite of the growing strength of the German Navy and Admiral Fisher's continued moves to build up the Royal Navy, the Liberal Government was still bent on making economies with the service Estimates. In the 1907–1908 Estimates yet another dreadnought was dropped from the programme planned by Lord Cawdor. Before the Estimates were presented, however, the Prime Minister had asked the First Lord, Lord Tweedmouth, if he would be prepared to accept a 50% reduction in the dreadnought programme. Very grudgingly the Board of Admiralty agreed to this proposed cut which led to a furious outcry in the press. On presenting the Estimates, however, Lord Tweedmouth said that if no satisfactory agreement could be reached at the Hague on the question of disarmament, then instead of the two dreadnoughts proposed, three would be built. The talks came to nothing, and so the Government gave the

Admiralty permission to construct the extra dreadnought. The three vessels of the 1907–1908 Programme were the *Collingwood*, *St. Vincent* and *Vanguard*, all sister ships and practically repeats of the *Bellerophon* class, except for the 12in gun which was a 50 calibre weapon and not 45 calibres.

The 1908–1909 Estimates saw yet another reduction to the dreadnought programme when only the *Neptune* and the battlecruiser *Indefatigable* were ordered. The *Indefatigable* was just an improved *Invincible*, with a better siting arrangement for the guns which improved the range of fire. The *Neptune* also had her main armament arranged differently from earlier dreadnoughts. The siting was to a certain extent influenced by the designs of vessels under construction for the American, Argentine and Brazilian navies. This led to a compromise between the *Dreadnought* and *Invincible* designs, with the midships turrets sited *en echelon* so that all the main armament could bear on either broadside in a very wide arc. In addition to this the first of the after turrets was superimposed, the first time a turret was so sited on a British battleship. The Admiralty had also become aware of the possible part that "lighter-than-air" craft could play in a future war and in recognition of this the *Neptune* had the upper deck so built that it could withstand the explosion of small bombs dropped on it from a height.

In February 1908 Germany passed a new Navy Law which increased the rate of construction of dreadnought type warships to four each year, an increase of one over the previous Law. In addition the large cruisers of the 1900 Law were reordered as battlecruisers. This would give Germany a total of 58 dreadnought type battleships and battlecruisers as opposed to 38 dreadnought type warships and twenty armoured cruisers. The publication of these facts led to a vigorous press campaign throughout Great Britain with the Conservative press demanding that six dreadnoughts be ordered in the 1909 Estimates. Admiral Fisher when presented with the figures of Germany's dreadnought construction at once requested eight dreadnoughts, but the First Lord, Reginald McKenna (who had replaced Lord Tweedmouth when Sir Henry Campbell Bannerman died in 1908 and was succeeded by Herbert Asquith as Prime Minister), only pressed for six. With the Admiralty undecided as to how many dreadnoughts should be ordered, the Chancellor of the Exchequer—Winston S. Churchill, at once asked to inspect the Admiralty's figures of the estimated rate of expansion of the German Navy. These had been computed to be 17 and possibly 21 dreadnoughts in commission by 1912. After close scrutiny it was felt that the Admiralty had overestimated the rate at which Germany could build dreadnoughts, and the Liberal Government, feeling there was no need for a rushed programme of construction would only agree to the construction of four dreadnoughts under the 1909 Estimates. They did, however, insert a clause to the effect that if it was felt necessary for the national security then a further four dreadnoughts could be constructed under the 1909 Estimates.

This led to further outbursts of angry comment, especially among those who agitated for a large navy, among them a number of influential Conservatives. It was at this time that the famous phrase "We want eight and we won't wait" was first coined. The Government was not to be shaken in its resolve and the Estimates remained at four dreadnoughts, with a further four conditional vessels.

The controversy over the dreadnought programme gave rise to a number of fortuitous side effects among which was an offer by the Australian and New Zealand Governments to provide funds for the construction of two extra dreadnoughts for the Royal Navy. The offers were accepted and led to the construction of the *Australia* and *New Zealand*, sister ships to the *Indefatigable*. Another side effect, which was to prove helpful in the future, was that with all the publicity concerning the German Navy Laws and a number of novels in which future wars were described, the general public became indoctrinated to the fact that war with Germany sometime in the future was certainly a possibility.

TABLE 4

Rate of construction 1905–1910

Year laid down	Dreadnoughts		Battlecruisers	
	Germany	Great Britain	Germany	Great Britain
1905		1		
1906		1		3
1907	4	3		
1908	3	2	1	
1909	2	4	2	2
1910	3	3		3
Ships laid down by 1912	12	14	3	8
Ships completed by 1912	10	14	3	8

The first four vessels of the "We want eight" programme were the *Colossus, Hercules, Lion* and *Orion.* They were laid down almost immediately in the summer of 1909, about three months before work would normally have begun on them. In the spring of the following year it was decided to lay down the four conditional vessels—the *Conqueror, Monarch,*

Princess Royal and *Thunderer*. The *Colossus* and *Hercules* were practically repeats of the *Neptune* excepting that the after tripod was suppressed, it being seriously affected by the smoke from the funnels. It was also found to be unnecessary for supporting the wireless aerials, just a short mast aft proving satisfactory for this purpose. The *Lion* and *Orion* of the first group were classed as super dreadnoughts, being armed with a new 13.5in gun instead of the 12in of the earlier dreadnought type vessels.

TABLE 5

Comparison of main armament 1905

Calibre	Length	Weight	Weight of shell	Maximum penetration of Krupp cemented armour at 5000yd
Watts				
13.5	45-cal	80 tons	1250lb	22in
12in	50-cal	58 tons	850lb	19in
12in	45-cal	50 tons	850lb	17½in
Barnaby				
13.5	30-cal	67 tons	1250lb	9in

The new 13.5in gun was a vast improvement on the model fitted in the earlier *Royal Sovereign* class, the great advantage being its greatly increased penetration capabilities. The *Orion* was the first vessel to carry the 13.5in which was sited in a different way from the earlier dreadnoughts. In the *Orion* all the main armament was sited along the keel line, as in the American vessels, instead of *en echelon*, as previously adopted in the Royal Navy. To a certain extent this was a necessary improvement forced upon the Admiralty in order to prevent serious strains being set up if the guns should fire across the deck. In addition to this it allowed far greater fire power to be developed, and the new arrangement was soon adopted for other vessels in the Royal Navy.

The *Orion*, together with the three vessels of the conditional order, the *Conqueror*, *Monarch* and *Thunderer* formed another new class of super-dreadnoughts, while the *Lion*, *Princess Royal* (the remaining vessel of the conditional order) and the *Queen Mary* (ordered under the 1910 Programme) were battlecruisers mounting eight of the new 13.5in guns. A number of minor problems were encountered with the *Lion*, including some necessary repairs to the turbines which somewhat delayed her completion. Another of the problems was the heat generated in the fore funnel, which was so great that the fire control position on the tripod mast sited just behind it became untenable, and navigating instruments were damaged. Before she was finally accepted into service the *Lion* had the forward tripod removed and replaced by a light mast, the bridge much enlarged and placed behind the conning tower, the fore funnel sited further aft and the height of all funnels increased.

By 1908 the Fisher-Beresford feud had become so subversive that it was endangering the morale of the whole service and the press was continually calling for someone to take a hand in the affair and bring it to a close, one way or another. The opposite occurred, and the row became more intense, those unfortunate enough to take sides sometimes falling foul of the contestants and having their careers hindered. One of these was Admiral Scott, who disagreed with Lord Beresford over a signal made during manoeuvres in 1908. Had he carried out his orders from Lord Beresford a collision would have resulted, so Admiral Scott refused to obey the order. A first class quarrel ensued and in the end Admiral Scott was moved to another command. Lord Beresford himself was also highly insubordinate, continually questioning orders from the Admiralty, criticising Admiralty policy and orders, and generally being completely tactless. He was absolutely opposed to the First Sea Lord and his reforms, and the incidents became so bitter between the two that discipline within the navy was seriously threatened. Admiral Fisher's reorganisation of the Home Fleet was the final blow. Up to 1909 Lord Beresford had held command of the Channel Fleet, but in 1909 this was united with the Home Fleet under one command and Lord Beresford was finally told to haul down his flag (SEE APPENDIX 2). Lord Beresford retired from the service a full two years before his due date, but once a free man and no longer hidebound by service discipline, he freely spoke his mind to all and sundry, condemning Admiral Fisher and Admiralty policy over the inadequate state of the navy, poor strategy, bad composition and disposition of the fleets, lack of war plans, insufficient cruisers and destroyers and many other minor points.

These disclosures, at first made privately by Beresford to the Prime Minister, Herbert Asquith, forced the Government, with the First Lord's agreement, to form a sub-committee of the Committee of Imperial Defence to investigate Lord Beresford's accusations in private. The formation of the committee infuriated Admiral Fisher who thereon threatened resignation, but was persuaded to remain, finally saying "I am not going till I am kicked out".

At the same time as the inquiry began some of Beresford's supporters published a series of letters from a Captain Bacon in the Mediterranean to

Admiral Fisher which complained of the handling of the Mediterranean Fleet. As a result of the publication of these letters and the outcry from the papers and the general public, Admiral Fisher was finally forced to resign from the Admiralty. The report of the inquiry published in August 1909 showed that Admiralty policy had not at any time placed the country's safety in jeopardy.

In the five years he had been in office as First Sea Lord, Admiral Fisher had completely revitalised the Royal Navy, set on foot many reforms and thoroughly prepared the service for the great struggles that lay ahead. He was succeeded in office by his staunch supporter Admiral Sir Arthur K. Wilson.

With the coming of the dreadnought era, the Admiralty concentrated all its efforts on the construction of large armoured ships. Small craft were not completely neglected though, as it was realised that the torpedo was a powerful weapon and the Admiralty did not want the navy to be left too far behind in the development of small torpedo craft. Vessels of the second-class cruiser type were omitted completely from the Estimates. This state of affairs was not to last, however, for German construction of this type of vessel grew to such proportions that there were many in the Admiralty who became alarmed that the Royal Navy had nothing with which to oppose these smaller cruisers. Consequently in the 1908–1909 Estimates five protected cruisers of the *Bristol* class were ordered. Although the specifications only asked for a speed of 25 knots, all the vessels exceeded 26 knots on trials. In the Estimates for the following year (1909–1910) four similar vessels of the *Weymouth* class were ordered. This was a slightly larger class and mounted a standard armament of eight 6in as opposed to the mixed armament of two 6in and ten 4in of the *Bristol* class.

In 1906 the first of a new standard design of destroyers was laid down, and known as the *Tribal* class. Between 1906 and 1910 a total of twelve of these vessels were built, all reaching a speed of 33 knots on fuel oil only. The first five vessels carried an armament of five 12-pdr and two 18in torpedo tubes and the remainder of the class had two 4in in place of the 12-pdr.

In 1908–1909 the Admiralty sought ways to avoid having two classes of vessel engaged in rather similar duties, and in an attempt to stem the duplication of torpedo boats and torpedo boat destroyers, designed an intermediate type of vessel that could cover the duties of both types of vessel. This led to the design of the *Beagle* class destroyers of about 900 tons and armed with one 4in and three 12-pdr and two 18in torpedo tubes.

Speed was reduced to 27 knots and it was decided to revert to coal for firing the boilers instead of the more costly oil. This decision was made as reports on comparable new German vessels showed that they were capable of steaming at speeds very much the same as our oil fired vessels, and the German vessels were coal fired. Added to this Britain had an abundant supply of very good coal in Wales, which was far cheaper than transporting oil from the Middle East. The *Beagle*'s were followed by the twenty vessels of the "*H*" class ordered under the 1909–1910 Programmes. These vessels were slightly smaller than the *Beagle*'s, but were rather better armed, carrying two 4in instead of one. The contract speed of 27 knots remained the same but the radius of action was increased by 200 miles.

In 1907 a new type of submarine entered service being a development of the earlier "*C*" class, which was still under construction. Known as the "*D*" class these vessels were almost double the size of the "*C*" class, displacing about 600 tons submerged. The surface speed was increased to 16 knots and three torpedo tubes were fitted. The "*D*" class differed radically from the previous classes in that they were fitted with main ballast tanks outside the hull, instead of internally as before. The shape of the hull itself was also altered, mainly so that the vessels could be powered by twin screws instead of the single screw of earlier vessels. These were driven by vertical four cycle diesel engines, first experimentally fitted in *A 13*. Earlier vessels had been equipped with a horizontal petrol engine.

D 1 made history when she was experimentally fitted with wireless telegraphy. The remaining seven vessels of the class proved more successful than *D 1*, displacement being increased slightly and the horsepower raised from 1200 to 1750. It had been intended to build a total of nineteen vessels of the "*D*" class, but while they were under construction an improved type of submarine was designed and superceded the "*D*" class.

CHAPTER 5

The Road to War

Rule Britannia, Britannia rules the waves
DR. ARNE

UNDER THE 1911 Programme another battlecruiser of the *Lion* class was planned, but when in January 1911 the Japanese ordered from Vickers the battlecruiser *Kongo* the Admiralty began to have doubts about the wisdom of ordering another vessel to the *Lion* design. The *Kongo* had much better protection than the *Lion*, and was the first foreign battlecruiser to mount a gun heavier than 12in. The siting of the four turrets, the secondary armament and the design generally gave the Admiralty much food for thought concerning their own designs. With such a superior vessel under construction the British battlecruiser was redesigned, the original plans for 85000 horsepower being raised to 108000, increasing the speed by about two knots. The initial design was approved in August 1911 and the final drawings in December of that year. The new battlecruiser was finally laid down in June 1912, and when war broke out in August 1914 the workers at John Brown's shipyard where she was under construction worked round the clock to speed her completion. She was the largest and fastest warship afloat and the only battlecruiser to mount 6in guns as secondary armament. Not only was the *Tiger* as the new vessel was named, an extremely well built vessel but she was also the last to be built to satisfy the sailors ideal of what a ship should look like. The design, being influenced by the *Kongo*, Q turret was placed behind the after funnel instead of in front of it, as in the *Lion*. This move had the effect of increasing the arc of fire of Q turret to 60 degrees before the beam and 90 degrees after it on either side.

In 1911 Anglo-German relations took a turn for the worse. Tension arose, when, in the spring of 1911 the French were forced to send troops to Fez in Morocco to put down a revolt against the Sultan. This was the first of a series of French moves aimed at annexing Moroccan territory. In retaliation, and without any real motives, except to create a rift in the

54

Entente Cordiale and cause a war, the Germans laid claim to the port of Agadir and its surrounding area, on the Atlantic coast of Morocco. The British Government was unable to perceive any purpose in the German move and could not extract a satisfactory answer from the Germans as to their intentions. The Liberal Government was split over the issue and no one knew, if it came to the test, whether the Government would be united in its condemnation of German policy. Both the Home Secretary, Winston Churchill, and Chancellor of the Exchequer—Lloyd George, were pacifist in their outlook, but after a period of uncertainty Lloyd George with the consent of the Prime Minister—Mr. Asquith, and the Foreign Secretary, Mr. Grey, took the bull by the horns and on July 21, 1911, at an after dinner speech at the Bankers' Association, made the statement—"If the situation were forced upon us in which peace could only be preserved by the surrender of the great and beneficient position Britain has won by centuries of heroism and achievement by allowing Britain to be treated, where her interests were vitally affected, as if she were of no account in the Cabinet of Nations, then I say emphatically that Peace at that price would be a humiliation intolerable for a great country like ours to endure."

The speech caused an uproar in Germany and the First Lord, told of the German reaction to the speech warned the Royal Navy of the possibility of war. It was indeed most fortunate that war was not declared, nor that the Germans made any surprise attack on the navy, for on the days following Lloyd George's speech the First Sea Lord, in spite of the continual warnings from the Foreign Secretary, remained totally unconvinced of the possibility of war. The Atlantic Fleet was in the North of Scotland while the First Division of the Home Fleet was at its base in Ireland. The Second Division was at Portland with its crews on four days leave and boilers shut down, and not even the torpedo nets were put out as a precaution. The Third and Fourth Divisions were at their various bases around the coasts with only their nucleus crews on board. In addition to this there was a strike in South Wales and there was no coal available for the Fleet!

The situation gradually eased, and the German Navy continued its programme of expansion, much to the anxiety of many in the Admiralty. The *Entente Cordiale* remained intact and in November an agreement was finally signed with Germany recognising French claims in Morocco in return for which a large part of the French Congo was handed over to Germany.

As a result of the Agadir crisis the Prime Minister convened a special meeting of the Committee of Imperial Defence on August 23, 1911, in order to discuss the plans of the Army and Navy in case of war with

Germany. At the morning seminar the Army put forward the probable moves of the German Army, and the British counter moves. In the afternoon the First Sea Lord, Sir Arthur Wilson, outlined the Navy's proposed operations in case of war. At once it became obvious that opinions differed, the Admiralty feeling that a close blockade of German ports would suffice to force the Germans to surrender. The Admiralty looked on the General Staff plans of the Army for sending an expeditionary force to France as unnecessary, preferring to have such a force ready for a surprise landing on the German coast. The Army, however was absolutely opposed to this plan.

With the two services at variance the Secretary of State for War, Mr. Haldane, threatened to resign from the War Office unless the Board of Admiralty formed a Naval War Staff to co-ordinate plans with the General Staff. Admiral Wilson, like his predecessor, Admiral Fisher, and also the First Lord, McKenna, found the proposals for the formation of a Naval Staff completely unacceptable.

However, there were others who also had their doubts about the wisdom of the Admiralty's policies of close blockade, and among these was Winston Churchill, who also favoured the formation of a War Staff. With the Agadir crisis abating and the apparent lack of Admiralty plans and poor relations with the General Staff, the Prime Minister decided that it was time there were changes at the Admiralty. As a result he asked Winston Churchill if he would like to be the new First Lord. Churchill accepted and he and McKenna (who privately did not readily accept the arrangement) exchanged offices in October 1911.

On taking office, Churchill, like Admiral Fisher, at once put in hand sweeping reforms. His first task was to set up the Naval War Staff, which so many of his colleagues in the Cabinet had urged the previous First Lord to do. The new staff was made up of three sections—operations, intelligence and mobilisation. It was found, however, that there were not enough officers with specialised knowledge to man the War Staff and so in 1912 the Staff College was set up at Portsmouth to train officers for the War Staff. Next on the list for reform were the Admiralty plans for war, which it seemed, had always been kept in Admiral Wilson's head. The plans for close blockade of Germany in particular were closely scrutinised. To enforce this close blockade of the Heligoland Bight destroyer flotillas three or four times the size of the German flotillas would be needed, and Britain just did not have that number of destroyers. Consequently existing flotillas were allocated to the task, with their strengths reduced by two-thirds, as while part of the force was on patrol there were always two other parts returning from and going out to the patrol area. This was a most unsatisfactory arrangement and Churchill insisted that the navy institute a system of distant blockade with the Home Fleet, based upon the new base of Scapa Flow and a barrage of destroyers situated across the straits of Dover supported by older battleships and minefields.

At the same time the Fleets were reorganised so that the number of vessels immediately ready for action was increased. Measures were also taken to guard against surprise attacks. To carry out the reforms as directed, Churchill appointed a new Board of Admiralty with Sir Francis Bridgeman late Commander-in-Chief of the Home Fleet as First Sea Lord, and Prince Louis of Battenburg as Second Sea Lord. Sir George Callaghan was appointed Commander-in-Chief of the Home Fleet and John Jellicoe as his Second-in-Command.

With the Agadir crisis over Lloyd George adopted a more conciliatory attitude towards Germany and talks between Britain and Germany were opened with a view to ending the naval rivalry between the two countries. Basically the terms the Kaiser was asked to agree to were—the acceptance of British supremacy at sea; no increase in the size of the German Navy programmes, and if at all possible a reduction; British recognition of German Colonial aims; and proposals for mutual declarations that the two countries would not formulate treaties or plans that could be considered aggressive to each other. The Kaiser's reply to these proposals was to send the Prime Minister the plans of the new 1912 Navy Law. Churchill, after studying the proposed Navy Law, was greatly perturbed. The planned programmes of British dreadnought construction allowed for a total of 4, 3, 4, 3, 4, 3, over the following six years as against a German output of 2, 2, 2, 2, 2, 2. The new German Navy Law, however, increased this rate of construction to 3, 2, 3, 2, 3, 2, which meant that if Britain was to maintain a superiority of 60% in dreadnoughts, as had been planned, then the Admiralty's rate of construction would have to be increased to 5, 4, 5, 4, 5, 4, over the next six years. Neither was this all, for the new German Navy Law also planned for the formation of a third dreadnought squadron in full commission. This posed a very serious threat to the Royal Navy's supremacy in its present state. The First Lord suggested that if the Germans were to arrange to complete their proposed programme in twelve years instead of six, then it would be possible to resume more cordial relations. It might also be possible then for Britain to reduce her planned rate of dreadnought construction. The First Lord was convinced that an attempt at mutual agreement on these terms should be made and that if successful then we might, as a result, achieve twelve years of peace.

The Secretary of State for War left London in February 6, 1912, with the proposals and returned two days later with a promise from Admiral Tirpitz that Germany would cancel the construction of one of her dreadnoughts. The British Government in a return gesture sacrificed two planned dreadnoughts, leaving our declared programme at 4, 5, 4, 4, 4, 4. The figure for the first year was, however, increased to five again when the Federated States of Malaya made a gift to the British Government for the construction of a *Queen Elizabeth* class battleship.

The formation of the third German dreadnought squadron forced the Admiralty to hurry up their reorganisation of the Fleets. Previously the Home and Atlantic Fleets had been available for Home defence. These were reorganised into three Fleets with a total of eight battle squadrons each of eight battleships, supported by cruisers and destroyers. The First Fleet had the Fleet Flagship and four battle squadrons each fully in commission. To achieve this strength the former Atlantic Fleet was based on home ports instead of at Gibraltar as hitherto, and the Mediterranean Fleet moved from Malta to Gibraltar. To compensate the Mediterranean Fleet for the loss of its *King Edward* battleships the Second Battlecruiser Squadron and the First Armoured Cruiser Squadron were allocated to the Mediterranean. In addition another dreadnought squadron was earmarked for the Mediterranean by 1915 to counter the threat posed by the growing Austrian Navy. The two battle squadrons of the Second Fleet, although fully commissioned, only had 60% of their complements on board, the remainder being under training or on courses ashore. The Third Fleet, also of two battle squadrons and five cruiser squadrons was formed of the older classes of warships and manned by care and maintenance parties. This Fleet could not be fully commissioned until after mobilisation of the reserves had been carried out. To speed up mobilisation of the Third Fleet a special reserve, the Immediate Reserve, was formed of men who were given periodic training and higher pay. They were liable to be called up before a general mobilisation was ordered. This reorganisation brought the strength of fully commissioned battleships to 49 as opposed to the German increase of 17 to 25. After mobilisation Britain would put to sea 65 battleships and Germany only 38.

The year of 1912 was certainly a momentous one for the Royal Navy. Apart from all the reorganisation and new warships coming into service a new branch of the navy was begun. The new heavier than air machine had proved itself and in January, Lieutenant C. R. Samson flew an aircraft off from a wooden platform sited on the foredeck of the *Africa*. The aircraft was a modified Short S 27 pusher biplane. The following May Lieutenant

Gregory repeated the experiment in front of the King during a review of the Fleet in Weymouth Bay. This time the aircraft took off from the *Hibernia* which was steaming at 10½ knots. After this successful beginning the new aircraft arm fell into decline and it wasn't until 1914 when the war started, that enthusiasm for the new form of warfare was again aroused. In the meantime four officers were sent on a flying training course and a number of experiments were conducted with the old cruiser *Hermes*. In 1913 she was fitted with a short flight deck and seaplanes launched from wheeled trolleys which fell into the sea when the aircraft became airborne. Progress was painfully slow, however, and by the start of the war only methods for launching aircraft had been experimented with. To land, aircraft were still ditched in the sea alongside the parent ship, floating on air cushions, and then hoisted back on board by cranes. A slow and clumsy operation.

At first the aircraft and pilots formed part of the Royal Flying Corps, but in July 1914 the naval section broke away and formed the Royal Naval Air Service.

Under the 1912 Programme, the basis of which had already been agreed when Churchill took over as First Lord, the Admiralty were to construct three battleships, one battlecruiser, three cruisers, and twenty destroyers. The designs for the battleships had all been prepared and just awaited a final signature before being presented to Parliament. However, uncertainty hung over the three battleships of the *Queen Elizabeth* class. Already Japan and America had battleships mounting 14in guns under construction. The Royal Navy had increased the calibre of its main armament once from 12in to 13.5in and there were some who felt it was time that the Admiralty raised the calibre again. There were, however, formidable problems to be overcome if the size of the guns were to be increased. To carry a 15in gun, which was the next satisfactory calibre, meant that the *Queen Elizabeth* class battleships would have to be increased in size, and they would thus cost more money. Also there could be no delay in having the guns and mountings ready or else completion of the ships would be delayed. The First Lord decided that the risks must be taken and so the requisite number of 15in guns were ordered for the new battleships, without first having constructed a model and having it thoroughly tested. The ordnance factory did, however, manage to hurry construction of one gun, and complete it four months ahead of the remainder. A number of basic tests were carried out on this gun to enable range tables, etc. to be made up. The tests showed the gun to be satisfactory in every way, with a much longer life than the 13.5in.

TABLE 6

Comparison of 13.5in and 15in guns

Calibre	Length	Weight	Weight of shell	Muzzle Velocity	Muzzle Energy
15in	42-cal	97 tons	1920lb	2450ft/sec	84070ft-tons
13.5in	45-cal	80 tons	1250lb	2500ft/sec	63190ft-tons

The initial plans for the *Queen Elizabeth* class allowed for a vessel mounting ten of the new guns, but it was seen that if the vessel only mounted eight such guns the broadside would still be heavier than ten 13.5in guns. If therefore the midships turret was dispensed with then the space thus saved could be used for extra boiler rooms which would enable the vessel to achieve a higher speed. With an extra four or five knots these battleships would be able to turn the van of the German Fleet and destroy the head of the line, enabling the slower British vessels to systematically destroy the enemy's rear line. The First Sea Lord felt that vessels built to this design were of far greater value than the battlecruisers and said that—"If it is worth while to spend far more than the price of your best battleship upon a fast heavily gunned vessel, it is better at the same time to give it the heaviest armour as well (the Queen Elizabeth class battleships had armour belts of 13in, the heaviest of any ship then afloat). You then have a ship which may indeed cost half as much again as a battleship, but which at any rate can do everything . . . The battlecruiser in other words should be superseded by the fast battleship". The War College felt that for the Royal Navy to maintain an advantage over the High Seas Fleet of 1914 a speed of 25 knots would be necessary. It was impossible to achieve speeds of this nature using coal fired boilers, and the only other alternative which would give this speed was oil. Until then only destroyers had been fitted with fully oil fired boilers, larger vessels still being coal fired but using oil to spray on the coal to assist with combustion. To go completely over to oil fired boilers for the new battleships would create many problems, not the least of which would be supply and transport of the fuel and the high cost of the initial outlay of the storage facilities and purchase, etc. The plunge was taken and the *Queen Elizabeth* class completed with fully oil fired boilers. At the same time an agreement with the Anglo-Persian Oil Company was concluded at a cost of £2m (later increased to £5m) and a controlling share in oil properties obtained which later led to a considerable reduction in the price the Admiralty had to pay for oil. The success of this operation was mainly due to the Commission on Oil which the First Lord set up under the leadership of Admiral Fisher.

The *Queen Elizabeth* class was followed by the five vessels of the *Revenge* class ordered under the 1913 and 1914 Programmes. Again these vessels were to mount the new 15in gun, but otherwise were merely enlarged editions of the *Iron Duke*. Protection was to a certain extent improved, and the *Ramillies* was additionally fitted with shallow external bulges, the first British battleship so fitted. Although the decision had been taken to give the *Queen Elizabeth*'s oil fuel, there were doubts as to the reliability of the supply should there be a war. In consequence it was decided that the *Revenge* class should revert to the use of coal for fuel, but this retrograde step was averted when Admiral Fisher returned to the Admiralty in October 1914 and rescinded the order.

Although the programme of dreadnought construction was deemed a wise move by the majority, it did give rise to many problems within the navy. So much effort was concentrated on the construction of dreadnought type vessels that certain other categories of warship fell into decline. Apart from this there was soon a serious manpower shortage in the navy, especially in the officer branches. This had been accentuated by the growth of the submarine arm and the rise of the Dominion navies, to which large numbers of officers were seconded for training purposes. To overcome the manpower problems a supplementary scheme of entry was begun in March 1913. With the new scheme it was hoped that boys between the ages of $17\frac{1}{2}$ and $18\frac{1}{2}$ from the Public Schools would be encouraged to enlist in the officer category. On joining they would be given an intensive training course lasting 18 months during which time they would receive a thorough grounding in seamanship both in the naval colleges ashore and on sea going warships in commission.

Vast sums of money had already been expended on the navy and in the Autumn of 1913 the First Lord requested that the annual manoeuvres planned for 1914 should be cancelled on the grounds of economy. Instead the First Sea Lord was asked if all the reserve ships and men of the Third Fleet could be mobilised as they would be in case of war. It was then planned that towards the end of 1914 all the Royal Naval Volunteer Reserve men should be mobilised and embark for a weeks training cruise on the vessels of the First Fleet.

Meanwhile in Europe the political situation had been rapidly deteriorating. At the end of June 1914 two squadrons of the Royal Navy were on official visits to Kronstadt and Kiel. While the Kaiser was inspecting the units at Kiel news was received of the assassination of the Emperor of

Austria—Franz Joseph. In an air of impending doom the regatta at Kiel was quickly brought to a close and the units returned to England.

While Europe tottered on the brink of war and statesmen hurried to and fro between the different embassies in an effort to avert a catastrophe, the mobilisation of the Reserve Fleet commenced on July 15. All the vessels of the Third Fleet coaled and raised steam, leaving soon after for a grand review at Spithead where they were to be inspected by the King. The morning after the review, July 19, the Third Fleet put to sea for exercises, dispersing to their home ports to pay off on July 23. That same day Austria-Hungary gave Serbia a 48 hour ultimatum, which was rejected on July 26. Fortunately only the smaller vessels of the Third Fleet had by then demobilised, and with the situation critical the First Sea Lord, Prince Louis of Battenberg, cancelled the order for the Third Fleet to demobilise. By July 28, when Austria declared war on Serbia, the Royal Navy had been put on a war footing. The following day, July 29, when the Austrians bombarded Belgrade, the First Fleet sailed from Portland for its new war base in Scapa Flow, passing the Straits of Dover during the night with all ships blacked out. By July 31 it was at its battle stations and the Second Fleet was busy assembling at Portland. On the evening of the Saturday, August 1, all the major powers were busy mobilising. The next day, Sunday, the Germans seized a number of British merchant ships at Kiel and with war now almost certain it was decided to replace the Commander-in-Chief of the First Fleet, George Callaghan, by Admiral Jellicoe, as the First Lord felt that Admiral Callaghan's health would not stand up to the strains of a war. By August 3 the mobilisation of all the Royal Naval forces was complete and the next day the Fleet was informed that the telegram ordering the commencement of hostilities against the Central Powers would be issued at midnight that night. Everything had been done, there was no surprise attack, and the Royal Navy was ready for its first major war since 1815.

The Board of Admiralty

First Lord	*Member of Parliament*	In overall charge of the Admiralty.
First Sea Lord	*Naval Post*	Responsible for the fighting and sea-going efficiency of the Fleet. Chief professional advisor of the First Lord.
Second Sea Lord	*Naval Post*	Responsible for the manning and training of all members of the Royal Navy.
Third Sea Lord	*Naval Post* (Also Controller of the Royal Navy)	Responsible for the design of all sea-going craft, aircraft and air-ships.
Fourth Sea Lord	*Naval Post*	Responsible for naval transport and stores.
First Civil Lord	*Member of Parliament*	Responsible for all shore works and buildings and also the Royal Hospital at Greenwich.
Second Civil Lord	*Member of Parliment* (Post created 1912 abolished 1917)	Responsible for handling contracts and dockyard business.
Parliamentary and Financial Secretary	*Member of Parliament* (Post abolished October 1959 and duties absorbed by Civil Lord)	Responsible for the Service Estimates.
Permanent Secretary	*Civil Post*	Responsible for general office organisation, procedure, precedent, etc.

Reorganisation of the Home Fleet March 1909

Nore Division	First Division	*Based at the Nore.*
Channel Fleet	Second Division	*Based at Portland.*
Nucleus Crew Vessels	Third Division ⎫	*Base at Portsmouth and*
Special Reserve Ships	Fourth Division ⎭	*Devonport.*
Atlantic Fleet		*Extension of the Home Fleet and based on the new port at Dover.*

The HOME FLEET was made up of 16 fully manned and 8 nucleus crew battleships, 10 fully manned and 10 nucleus crew armoured cruisers (including 3 battle-cruisers).

The ATLANTIC FLEET was made up of 6 battleships and 4 armoured crusiers.

Credits for Illustrations

Author's Collection: 67, 68 (upper), 70 (centre), 77 (foot), 81, 82 (lower), 84 (lower two), 85, 92 (upper two), 95, 99 (upper right), 100 (top), 103, 112 (lower), 113, 115, 123, 126, 136 (lower), 138 (upper left).

Crown Copyright: 140 (lower), 141 (upper).

Imperial War Museum: 65, 66, 71 (upper), 77 (centre), 83, 86 (upper), 87 (upper), 88, 90 (upper), 92 (foot), 94, 121, 143 (upper).

Mansell Collection: 73, 74 (lower), 77 (top), 86 (lower), 96, 97 (lower), 102, 116, 118, 122, 124 (upper), 141 (lower), 142, 143 (lower).

Tom Molland: 89 (upper), 98 (upper), 112 (upper), 124 (lower), 125 (top), 133 (upper).

National Maritime Museum: 70 (top), 79, 80 (upper), 89 (lower), 90 (lower), 98 (lower).

Radio Times Hulton Picture Library: 69, 72, 74 (upper), 75, 76, 78, 80 (lower), 87 (lower), 91, 93, 97 (upper), 99 (upper left), 99 (lower), 100 (lower two), 102 (inset), 104, 105, 108, 109, 110, 111, 119, 120 (upper), 129, 130, 132, 133 (lower), 135, 138 (upper right), 139 (upper), 140 (upper),144.

Real Photographs: 101 (upper), 114 (lower), 117 (centre), 125 (lower two), 127, 128 (lower), 131, 134 (upper), 136 (upper), 138 (foot).

P. A. Vicary: 68 (lower), 70 (foot), 71 (lower), 82 (upper), 84 (top), 106, 107, 114 (upper), 117 (top), 117 (foot), 120 (lower), 128 (upper), 134 (lower), 137, 139 (lower).

By the 1880s the warships of the Royal Navy were vastly different from those of 1816. Most vessels were now constructed of steel and although sails were still the main mode of propulsion, the steam engine was gradually taking over from the sail as the method of propulsion. Typical of a type of vessel having both steam and sail for propulsion was the steel hulled cruiser Comus *shown above.*

OPPOSITE, TOP: *One of the most significant developments of the 1880s was the reintroduction of the breech-loading gun. The illustration shows the experimental 43-ton 12in BLR.*

OPPOSITE, LEFT: *After an experimental 43-ton 12in gun had burst on trials, it was decided that future models should have additional strengthening. This new 12in 45-ton breech-loader now became the standard weapon of the Royal Navy's battleships. The illustration shows such a gun on the after barbette of the* Collingwood.

ABOVE: *The Controller of the Royal Navy at the time was Vice-Admiral Sir William Houston Stewart.*

LEFT: *Among the first vessels to carry the new 12in gun was the* Edinburgh, *completed in 1887. She was finally used as a target ship for testing armour-piercing shells.*

RIGHT: *In 1880, William Ewart Gladstone became Prime Minister. Having previously served as Chancellor of the Exchequer, his Government was noted for the extreme financial restrictions that it placed on the navy's expenditure.*

RIGHT: *The First Lord of the Admiralty under Gladstone was Sir Thomas George Baring, the First Earl of Northbrook. Resulting from the economic restrictions, programmes of naval construction and developments were seriously delayed.*

LEFT: *A far superior design to the* Edinburgh *was that of the* Collingwood *shown here. The armament was concentrated in batteries amidships.*

ABOVE: *One of the most unsatisfactory vessels ever completed for the navy was the* Imperieuse *together with her sister ship the* Warspite. *They were the last armoured vessels to be designed with a square rig. The illustration shows the* Imperieuse *after the removal of her rig following extensive trials.*

LEFT: *One of the best features of the* Imperieuse *was the fact that in action she had a broadside of three 9.2in and five 6in BL guns. The illustration shows one of the 6in guns.*

BELOW: *Following the success of the* Collingwood *design, it was decided to build a further four vessels to a very similar pattern. The illustration shows the* Camperdown *in 1889. Note the tall main mast with a semaphore arm, used for long-distance signalling.*

While the Admiral class of battleships, of
which the Camperdown *was one, were
under construction, a more powerful gun of
13.5in calibre had been designed. The
illustration shows the after-barbette of the*
Rodney (*the first ship of the Admiral class
to be completed*) *with two of the 13.5in
guns, and beside them a Gatling machine
gun. In the foreground is a 3-pdr machine
gun*

The fifth vessel of the Admiral class, the
Benbow, *was also to have mounted the
13.5in gun. Delays, however, in the
production of the gun resulted in the vessel
mounting a 16.25in gun. The illustration
shows the* Benbow *under construction at
the Thames Ironworks.*

ABOVE, LEFT: *From 1863 to 1879, the Khedive Ismail Pasha who ruled Egypt made great efforts at modernisation. As a result of this, he went bankrupt in 1876 and was succeeded by his weak son, Tewfik Pasha, in 1879. The illustration shows Ismail Pasha in the later years of his reign.*

ABOVE: *In 1881, Sayed Ahmed Arabi Pasha took control of Egypt and instigated a number of anti-European demonstrations. Believing that a combined British and French force was about to attack Egypt, he immediately set about fortifying the port of Alexandria.*

LEFT: *At the time of the Egyptian crisis, the Commander-in-Chief of the Mediterranean was Lord Alcestor, Admiral Frederick Beauchamp Paget Seymour. After a final ultimatum to Arabi Pasha to dismantle the forts of Alexandria, Admiral Seymour prepared his mixed squadron of both steam and sail vessels for action.*

RIGHT: *At 22.00 on July 10, 1882, the British squadron took up bombarding positions in the port of Alexandria. They cleared for action, striking topgallant masts and taking in their bowsprits. The vessels in the illustration are, from left to right:* Inflexible, Penelope, Temeraire, Alexandra, Monarch, Sultan *and* Invicible.

LEFT: *At 07.00 on July 11, the* Alexandra *fired the opening shot in the bombardment of Alexandria. The Flagship, the* Invincible, *hoisted the signal for general action.*

LEFT: *The British warships sustained little damage during the bombardment; the protection afforded by armour plate proving to be more effective than previous experiments had shown. The most seriously damaged vessel was the* Alexandra, *receiving over sixty hits. The illustration shows the explosion of a shell on the* Alexandra.

ABOVE: *One of the first tasks of the naval landing force was to take over the forts built by Arabi Pasha. The illustration shows such a fort overlooking the Port of Alexandria.*

BELOW: *On occupying the forts, one of the first tasks was to spike the guns, ensuring that they could not be used again. With some this proved to be unnecessary as the illustration of this muzzle-loader at Fort Pharos shows. During the bombardment, it suffered a direct hit.*

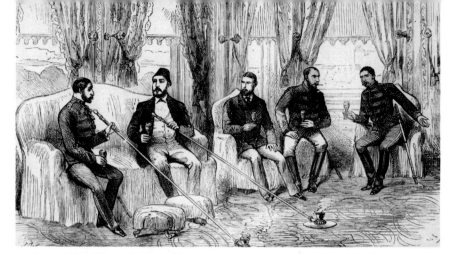

TOP: *On September 2, 1882, the Khedive Tewfik Pasha was reinstated as the ruler of Egypt. The illustration shows him smoking the pipe of peace with the Duke of Connaught.*

ABOVE: *Arabi Pasha finally surrendered to General Drury Lowe at Abassiyeh on September 14, 1882. The illustration shows from left to right: Colonel Stuart, Toulba Pasha, Arabi Pasha and General Drury Lowe.*

LEFT: *Following the Egyptian crisis, a revolt broke out under the leadership of the Mahai in the Protectorate of the Sudan. The British Army was hard-pressed to subdue the Dervishes and a Royal Navy squadron under Rear-Admiral Sir William Hewitt was sent to the Red Sea to protect British interests in the area.*

ABOVE: *By 1880, means of defence against torpedo attacks were becoming of paramount importance. At that time the only really satisfactory method was the torpedo net slung from booms braced from the sides of the ship. The illustration shows the Bullivant type of net in the course of being hung by the* Sultan. *It was constructed of steel rings 6½ inches in diameter connected by smaller rings. It extended below the water line to the depth of the hull.*

RIGHT: *Later types of torpedo net formed a skirt round the hull of the vessel. The illustration shows a type of net which was hung from booms which were nearly flush with the water line, the net extending about 25ft below the surface. With this type of net vessels could proceed about 3 knots.*

BELOW: *The torpedo had advanced greatly from the early Whitehead version. Its size had increased to 18in. In the illustration such a weapon is being prepared for firing.*

LEFT: *Such was the state of the navy in 1884 that a number of people felt that the true facts about the condition of the navy should be presented to the public. William Thomas Stead (editor of the Pall Mall Gazette), with the assistance of Captain Fisher, presented a series of articles in his magazine giving these figures just before the forthcoming General Election in 1884.*

RIGHT: *Following the Russian crisis of 1884, the Admiralty in 1885 formed the Particular Service Squadron to serve as a Baltic expeditionary fleet. The squadron was composed of obsolete vessels, quite unsuited for operating together as a homogeneous squadron. The squadron was not needed for active duties and was retained for trials purposes, being used as targets against which the new torpedo boats could practise battle manoeuvres. They were also used for the testing of mines, booms and torpedo nets. Typical of the vessels forming the squadron are the three shown opposite, from top to bottom they are:* Devastation, Sultan *and* Hotspur.

BELOW: *As a result of the series of articles in the* Pall Mall Gazette *Lord Northbrook instituted a new Five-year plan of construction. Included in the programme were the battleships* Sans Pareil *and* Victoria. *They had a unique silhouette with the secondary armament in batteries around the superstructure which extended right aft to the stern. There was just a single turret forward. The illustration shows the* Victoria *passing through the swing bridge at Newcastle-upon-Tyne.*

ABOVE: *Forming part of Lord Northbrook's Five-year plan of construction was a large order for cruisers. One of the classes ordered was the* River *class protected cruisers, armed with two 8in and ten 6in guns. The illustration shows the* Thames *in 1887.*

LEFT: *In 1886, Lord Salisbury became Prime Minister when Gladstone resigned. The new First Lord of the Admiralty (illustrated here) was Lord George Hamilton. During his term of office the Naval Defence Act was passed.*

RIGHT: *With Lord Hamilton as First Lord of the Admiralty, a new Board of the Admiralty was formed and the Chief Constructor, Barnaby, resigned. His place was taken by Mr. White, shown here.*

BELOW: *One of the vessels designed under Lord Northbrook's regime was the Nile. Later, however, when Mr. White became Chief Constructor, alterations were made to the design of the Nile.*

With great advances being made in
protection and gunnery, it was necessary to
continually test materials to ensure that they
were up to standard with modern technology.
To test new materials and weapons, the old
ironclad Resistance was fitted with special
armour plates and subjected to shell fire and
torpedo attacks. The first tests (illustrated
here) were carried out in 1887.

As in the old sailing days, the Victorian
officers were very fastidious about keeping
their warships in a high state of cleanliness.
The illustration shows a Petty Officer
instructing two sailors in their next task.

ABOVE: *Throughout the 19th century Burma had posed many problems for the British Government. In the early 1820s the Army had sent troops to the country to prevent the Burmese invading Bengal, and in 1852 Britain had been involved in the second Burma War, when the Irrawaddy Delta was annexed. Then, in 1885, the King of Burma confiscated the Bombay-Burma Company's property. At this, British and Indian troops were again called in and the small vessels of the Royal Navy supported the Army along the Irrawaddy River. The illustration shows a river gunboat on the Irrawady in 1886.*

BELOW: *For the Third Burma War the navy commandeered a number of small craft for use with the Irrawaddy Flotilla. The illustration shows the small vessel Kathleen armed with small cannon in the bow and stern. The sides of the vessel have been built up with bales to give protection against rifle fire.*

FOOT: *The British Army, with the help of the Irrawaddy Flotilla, eventually managed to take Mandalay, the capital of Burma. The King was deported and the rest of the country occupied, then becoming a province of the Indian Empire. The illustration shows sunken Burmese vessels along the shores of the Irrawaddy during the advance on Mandalay.*

ABOVE: *On March 6, 1889, the obsolete battleship* Sultan *grounded in the Comino Channel at Malta. She later sank but was raised in August 1889 and put into dock at Malta, where she was temporarily repaired before being brought home to Portsmouth where she was modernised. The illustration shows her just after grounding.*

LEFT: *Although mess decks in the Royal Navy were still very cramped, the food generally had greatly improved. The illustration shows a sailor carrying a side of beef down to a vessel's cold-store.*

BELOW: *In the accompanying illustration, the heads of the various messes are shown queueing up for their rations of meat.*

RIGHT: *One of the most important functions in the routine daily life on board a warship was the issue of the rum ration shown here.*

BELOW: *Although modern technology had greatly improved the state of the navy, obsolete weapons such as the cutlass were still considered necessary as part of a sailor's personal weapons. The illustration shows a sailor at cutlass drill practising movements against men armed with rifles and bayonets.*

RIGHT: *Much of the practical training was done on board vessels of the Royal Navy. In the illustration a group of young seamen are being given instruction in the art of "rope lore" on board the* Theseus.

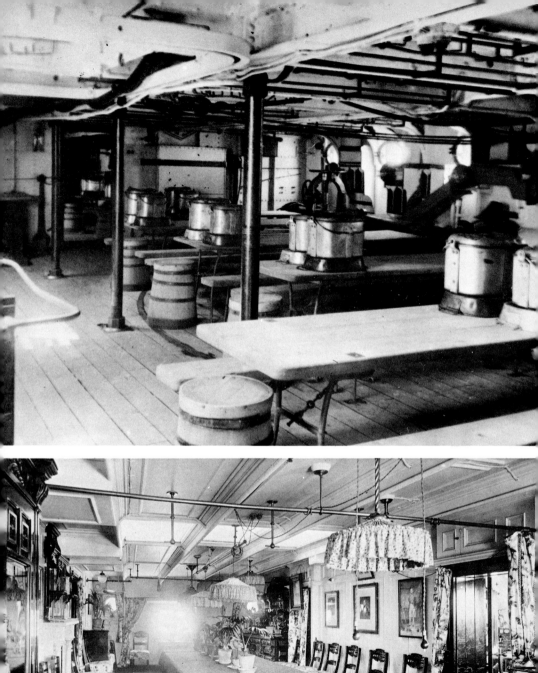

OPPOSITE, TOP: *Since the end of the Napoleonic Wars the conditions of service in the Royal Navy had greatly improved, but there was still room for more improvement. The most common criticism was lack of space and inadequate messing arrangements. The illustration shows a cramped mess deck on board the* Hero *in 1890.*

OPPOSITE, LEFT: *In stark contrast to the seamen's quarters were those of the officers. The illustration shows the officers' dining room on board the* Renown.

ABOVE: *Initial training of a seaman was still carried out on board old sailing vessels such as the* Impregnable *shown here in 1912. The illustration shows men being taught how to reef a sail.*

RIGHT: *In 1886, Lord Salisbury was returned to Parliament for the second time as Prime Minister. The illustration shows him in later life.*

With Lord Salisbury as Prime Minister, a new Naval Defence Act was passed, one of the first classes of warship to be designed under the Act being the Royal Sovereign *class battleships. The illustration of the* Repulse *in 1897 clearly shows the booms prominently stowed along the sides of the hull.*

Following the ordering of the Royal Sovereign *class battleships, two second class battleships were planned. Like many other battleships built at this time, the arrangement of the boiler rooms dictated the rather unusual side-by-side funnel arrangement. The illustration shows the* Barfleur *in 1895.*

The seven vessels of the Edgar class cruisers formed part of the large cruiser construction programme of the Naval Defence Act. The illustration is of the Edgar herself.

The Renown (shown here just after completion) was to have been the forerunner of a new class of battleship that was to carry a new 12in gun that was then under development. The completion of the gun was delayed and only one vessel of the class, the Renown, was ordered, being completed as a second class battleship, armed with 10in guns.

OPPOSITE, TOP: *One of the largest classes of cruisers ordered under the Naval Defence Act was the* Apollo *class. Shown here is the after 6in gun on the* Charybdis.

OPPOSITE, LEFT: *In November 1892 the battleship* Howe *grounded on Ferrol rock in the Mediterranean. As the illustration shows, the vessel had a severe list, making salvage a difficult operation. A Swedish firm finally refloated the* Howe *in March 1893.*

ABOVE: *By the 1890s, the torpedo boat had been greatly developed. One of the foremost men in the field of torpedo boat construction was Sir Alfred Yarrow, shown here when he was about 25.*

OPPOSITE, TOP: *To counter the threat of a new torpedo boat under construction in France, Yarrow built the torpedo boat* Havoc *at the request of Admiral Fisher.*

OPPOSITE, CENTRE: *At the same time, Yarrow also constructed the torpedo boat* Hornet, *fitted with a newly designed boiler. With this, she became the fastest vessel in the world, reaching a speed of 28 knots on trials.*

OPPOSITE, LEFT: *With the successful trials of* Havoc *and* Hornet *completed, the Admiralty ordered the thiry-six torpedo destroyers of the "A" class. These were of a similar design to that of the* Havoc.

ABOVE: *The Spencer programme of 1893, planned for a far greater rate of construction than the previous Naval Defence Act. The programme received its name from Lord Spencer* (above) *who felt that the Royal Navy was not nearly strong enough to counter the combined strengths of the French and Russian navies.*

ABOVE: *As with the Naval Defence Act, the Spencer Programme concentrated on the construction of cruisers. According to Lord Beresford, the number ordered was insufficient, and for reasons of economy, even* **this** *number was reduced. In the original Spencer plan, 12 second class cruisers of the* Talbot *class were to have been laid down, but only nine were ever ordered. The illustration of the* Talbot *shows in detail one of the eight 12-pdrs.*

BELOW: *One of the cruiser classes laid down under the Spencer Programme was seriously delayed, the first vessel not being put on the stocks until two years after the programme had been passed. The illustration of one of these vessels, taken on the forecastle of the* Diadem *in 1898, shows the two forward 6in guns.*

ABOVE: *As with all other battleships, the engines of the* Mars *were placed below armoured decks. The illustration shows the 12000ihp machines, constructed by Messrs. Laird, before installation in the* Mars.

RIGHT: *One of the new battleship classes ordered under the Spencer Programme was the* Majestic *class. The illustration shows the hull of the* Mars *on June 16, 1894, twelve days after the keel had been laid.*

BELOW: *On all large, modern warships of the Royal Navy is fitted a metalwork shop where all minor repairs to the ship and its machinery can be carried out. The illustration shows the "smithy" on board the* Majestic.

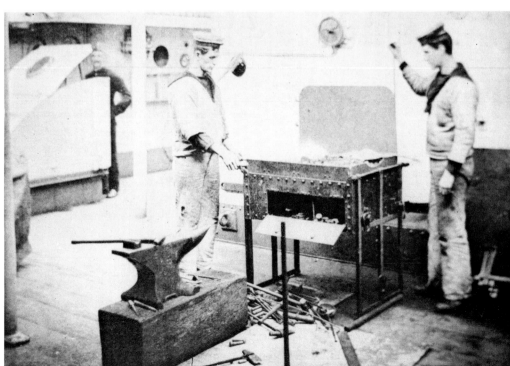

RIGHT: *The inevitable Court Martial inquiry into the loss of the* Victoria *placed the responsibility for the collision upon Admiral George Tryon, the Commander-in-Chief of the Mediterranean Fleet.*

LEFT: *On June 22, 1893, the Mediterranean Fleet suffered a disaster almost identical to the accident of September 1, 1875, when the* Iron Duke *rammed* Vanguard. *This time the* Camperdown *rammed the* Victoria *while conducting a turn during exercises. Following a nearly 70° impact, the sterns of the two vessels began to swing apart, enlarging the breach in the bow of the* Victoria. *As the vessels parted, the* Victoria *turned towards land, but, owing to the destruction of the watertight connection of the side plating of two important transverse bulkheads, the water flooded so many compartments that the vessel soon began to settle.*

BELOW: *The Court Martial felt unable to comment on the reasons for the capsizing of the* Victoria, *which was unfortunate as it led the general public to believe there were serious design faults in our warships. The accompanying sketch shows the Court Martial on the* Hibernia.

In 1894, the Powerful *class cruisers,
ordered under the Spencer Programme were
laid down. They were the largest cruisers
yet built for the navy and were only 200
tons lighter than the* Majestic *class
battleships built under the same programme.
The illustrations show (above) the* Terrible
and (below) Prince George of the Majestic
class.

ABOVE: *In 1896, when the Sultan of Zanzibar died, the Army revolted under the leadership of Prince Seyyid Khalid ben Barghash* (above).

BELOW: *With the full support of the army, Prince Khalid broke out his personal standard in the late Sultan's palace. In the illustration, the Government house is in the centre with the harem to the left and the Sultan's palace to the right.*

ABOVE: *The British Government ordered the Admiral commanding the South-African station, Admiral Sir Harry Rawson, to Zanzibar to restore order and replace the rightful heir on the Sultan's Throne.*

The Flagship of Admiral Rawson was the St. George, *and on August 28, 1896, she bombarded the rebel Prince in the Sultan's palace.*

When the bombardment began, the only vessel in the harbour was the Glasgow, *the late Sultan's yacht, which had been taken over by the rebel Prince. The* Glasgow (below) *was soon severely damaged.*

The bombardment, which lasted just over half an hour, destroyed the palace and harem and severely damaged a number of other buildings. Following this, the rebel Prince surrendered.

Under the 1897–1898 estimates the six armoured crusiers of the Cressy class were ordered. In many ways they were similar to the earlier Powerful class. The illustration shows the Euryalus in 1903.

In 1897, tribal wars broke out on the River Niger in West Africa. A naval landing force from Admiral Rawson's Squadron was landed to put down the rebellion. The illustration shows sailors and marines from the St. George in a skirmish on the road to Benin.

LEFT: *During the 1890s the Hon. Charles Parsons (see inset) worked steadily on the development of the steam turbine. In this field he became the world's leading authority. The vessel on which Parsons carried out many of his experiments with the steam turbine was aptly named* Turbinia. *She is shown here on high speed manoeuvres in 1894.*

ABOVE: *In 1895 the Conservatives under Lord Salisbury were returned to power for a third time. The new First Lord of the Admiralty—Mr. Goschen (above) who while realising the need to develop the navy, managed to do so successfully without any undue extravagance. This was not the first time that Goschen had served as First Lord of the Admiralty, previously having succeeded Sir Hugh Childers in 1871.*

OPPOSITE, TOP: *1897 was the Diamond Jubilee year of Queen Victoria's reign. In honour of the occasion the navy staged the largest assembly of warships in a fleet review that the world had ever seen. Line upon line of battleships with paintwork gleaming stretched as far as the eye could see.*

OPPOSITE, LEFT: *Steam pinnaces and whalers dashed to and fro between the lines of moored warships. As normal the warships were dressed overall with the crews lining the decks. In the picture a steam pinnace and a whaler are passing the battleship.*

ABOVE: *At the end of the lines of warships were moored hundreds of yachts gaily decorated in bunting.*

BELOW: *In the evening, after the review was over, the Fleet gave a spectacular show, the outline of the hull, superstructure and mast of every vessel being picked out in thousands of tiny lights.*

ABOVE: *In 1898 one of the oldest vessels in the Royal Navy was wrecked on Blackpool Beach. The* Foudroyant, *named after a French prize taken in 1758, had been launched in 1798. During the last years of her life she had served as a tender to the gunnery school* Cambridge, *being replaced by the* Trincomalee *in 1890.*

OPPOSITE, TOP: *In 1898 the* Viper, *a new torpedo boat destroyer developed by Parsons commenced her trials for the Royal Navy. The illustration shows her steaming at 36 knots.*

OPPOSITE, RIGHT: *While Parsons was developing the* Viper, *the shipbuilding firm of Armstrongs was designing as a private venture the* Cobra. *This torpedo boat destroyer was powered by steam turbines supplied by the firm of Parsons. The* Cobra, *however, was not built to quite the same high standard as the* Viper.

OPPOSITE, TOP: *In 1900 the Boxer Rising broke out in China and the vessels of the Royal Navy on the Chinese Station were called upon to supply landing parties to assist the army. The prelude to the rising was the siege of the legations in the capitol of Peking. The illustration shows the British legation under siege by the Boxers.*

OPPOSITE, LEFT: *At the mouth of the Peiho River a number of Chinese warships were captured and pressed into service with the Allied forces. The illustration shows a Chinese torpedo boat destroyer, renamed* Taku, *lying alongside the battleship* Centurion.

ABOVE: *With the legations in Peking cut off by the Boxers, the British Commander-in-Chief of the Chinese Station, Admiral Edward Seymour, together with the help of men sent by the French, Russians, Japanese and Germans tried to force a way through to the city. The Allies landed at the mouth of the Peiho River but were held by the Boxers at Tientsin. At one point a Chinese force of about 4000 attacked a combined British-German Force of 900 men. The fight lasted about two hours before the Chinese were finally driven off at Lang-Fang.*

OPPOSITE, TOP: *Soon, however, the Allies were forced to retreat to Tientsin. The railway line was abandoned, and the sailors carried the wounded back down the Peiho River in junks towed by Boxer prisoners.*

OPPOSITE, LEFT: *After receiving reinforcements Admiral Seymour recommenced his march on Peking from Tientsin. As they retreated, however, the Chinese destroyed the railway line, which was repaired by Royal Naval seamen in charge of Chinese working gangs.*

ABOVE: *Shown here are a group of officers from the different nationalities involved in the relief of the legations in Peking.*

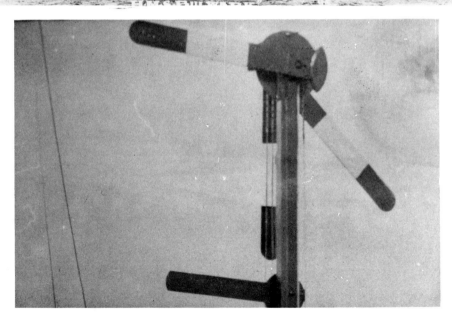

OPPOSITE, TOP: *The accompanying illustration of the* Bulwark *of the* London *class battleships ordered under the 1898–1900 Estimates shows up clearly many of the inventions evolved during the previous decade. In the bridge wings can be seen the new searchlights, and on the foremost the rudimentary fire-control position. On the after bridge wings can be seen the two semaphore masts.*

OPPOSITE, LEFT: *The normal means of intercommunication between warships in the 1890s was by means of the semaphore arm shown here. This means of communication was only possible over short distances, although to increase the range the arms were sometimes fitted at the top of the foremast.*

ABOVE: *For searching out the enemy at night the searchlight had been developed. The one above, shown on board the* Magnificent, *is worked by three dynamos, each of 600 amps. These searchlights were sited at strategic points around the warship.*

The first submarines to enter service with the Royal Navy were the five vessels of the Holland *type. The illustration shows vessels Nos. 2 and 5 alongside the depot ship* Thames *in 1906.*

Following the acceptance of the submarine as a vessel of war the navy developed further designs. The illustrations show (left) A3 (*sunk in a collision off the Isle of Wight in 1912*), (above) C15 *and* (below) D4. *The* D4 *was the first British submarine to be fitted with a gun, but the illustration was taken before this modification was made.*

ABOVE: *By 1900 the torpedo boat destroyer had become a highly developed weapon. The accompanying photograph taken early in 1900 shows torpedo boat destroyers on exercises with the battle fleet.*

OPPOSITE, TOP: *During exercises on August 3, 1901, the* Viper *ran aground on the Renonquet reef off the Casquets, Alderney, in dense fog. At the time she was steering a course to avoid an "enemy" torpedo boat destroyer, and jumping a ledge on the reef she ripped out her bottom.*

OPPOSITE, CENTRE: *Following the construction of the* London *and* Duncan *classes the Admiralty laid down the* King Edward VII *class battleships. The illustration shows the* Africa *(nearest the camera) with two other vessels of the class behind.*

OPPOSITE, RIGHT: *While the* King Edward VII *class was under construction a new class of destroyers, the* Rivers, *had been laid down. They differed from earlier classes in having a high forecastle deck instead of a turtleback construction. This picture of the* Rother *in 1907 shows the pronounced sheer aft and the depth of the new deck.*

LEFT: *In 1902 Admiral Fisher ended his term as Commander-in-Chief of the Mediterranean Station. The illustration shows the* Renown *(centre) with Admiral Fisher on board leaving Malta harbour for the last time. To the left is the* Bulwark.

ABOVE: *On returning to England from the Mediterranean Admiral Fisher was appointed Second Sea Lord. Until 1902, when he began to reorganise the training of officers in the navy. Until then all officer cadets had been given their initial two years training in the two wooden hulks* Britannia *and* Hindustan *moored at Dartmouth.*

ABOVE: *To replace the two old wooden hulks at Dartmouth Admiral Fisher built two new colleges. The first, Osborne, was built around the late Queen Victoria's country residence at Osborne in the Isle of Wight. Here cadets would spend the first two years of their naval career training.*

BELOW: *From Osborne the cadets then went to a new college at Dartmouth where they spent a further two years training. This new college was built on the slopes of the hill overlooking the site where the* Britannia *and* Hindustan *had been moored.*

OPPOSITE, TOP: *At the same time as the training of the officers of the Royal Navy was improving, Rear-Admiral Sir Percy Scott was improving the gunnery of the navy. He was instrumental in having the waste piece of ground at Whale Island reclaimed for a new gunnery school. Admiral Scott was also a great inventor developing the dotter, deflection teacher and loading tray all machines designed to improve gunnery.*

ABOVE: *When the new gunnery school at Whale Island was completed lessons were given in modern gunnery techniques, many of them developed by Admiral Scott. The class in the photograph is being instructed in the uses and construction of various types of ammunition.*

OPPOSITE, LEFT: *The targets used by Admiral Scott in his gunnery exercises were similar to the one shown in the photograph. By 1905 Admiral Fisher had managed to get the battleships using these targets at a range of between 5000 and 7000 yards, the gunnery having so much improved. In addition the targets were towed at a speed of about 15 knots and some vessels were managing to score many hits on the target with a high rate of fire. The target itself measured 90ft by 30ft.*

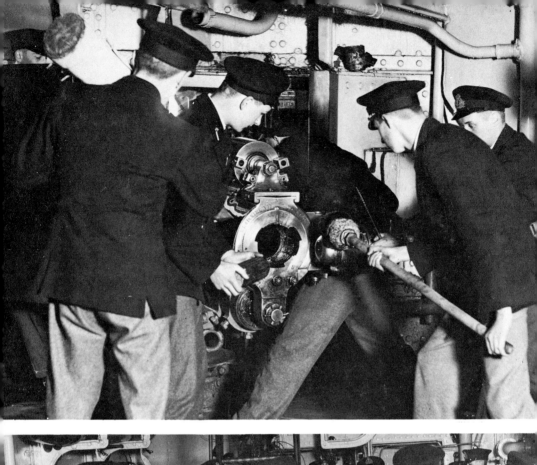

RIGHT: *While he was in charge of the gunnery school* Excellent, *Admiral Fisher opened a new school for mining and torpedo warfare. In the accompanying illustration a party of seamen are preparing a 72lb electro-contact mine. These mines were used for harbour defence being placed in a line across the harbour mouth and connected to the shore by an electrical circuit. The mines were only made live when an electrical circuit with the shore was completed when any ship then touching a mine would explode it. The normal explosive used in these mines was guncotton.*

LEFT: *The knowledge learnt at Whale Island was thus being put to great use. The photograph shows a practical lesson on board a training ship with cadets loading a 4in gun.*

BELOW, LEFT: *The training ship used in the photograph is the* Thunderer *and here cadets are being given instruction in the use of the torpedo.*

RIGHT: *Another branch of seamanship that was becoming highly developed in the navy was that of the diver. This branch called for men of high medical character and the work was often exacting and dangerous. Every vessel in commission carried a diver, and the one shown in the illustration belonged to the* Camperdown. *But for his helmet he was complete in his diving outfit.*

ABOVE: *In 1902 the Duke and Duchess of Connaught undertook a tour of the world aboard the battleship* Renown. *The illustration shows the* Renown *with the Royal couple aboard off Malta, escorted by torpedo boat destroyers.*

OPPOSITE, TOP: *In 1903 the Admiralty laid down the cruiser* Black Prince, *later sunk at the Battle of Jutland in the First World War. The design of the class was not a success.*

OPPOSITE, CENTRE: *The next class of cruisers to be laid down was the* Minotaur *class, of which the nameship is illustrated. The poor siting of the 6in battery in the* Black Prince *was altered the secondary guns in this class being mounted in turrets on the main deck where they were free from rough seas. In addition the calibre was increased to 7.5in.*

OPPOSITE, FOOT: *The* Lord Nelson *class of battleships were the next to be completed, and were easily recognisable for their high superstructure. The photograph shows the* Lord Nelson *before the height of her funnels was increased.*

BELOW: *In 1905 Admiral Fisher instituted regular Battle Practice for the Fleet. The illustration shows the* Illustrious *engaged in a practice shoot.*

ABOVE: *Much of the strength and high state of efficiency of the navy was due to the driving force of Admiral Fisher who put through many reforms and developments during his terms of office as First and Second Sea Lord.*

RIGHT: *In December 1906 Admiral Fisher's brainchild, the* Dreadnought, *entered service with the Royal Navy. At the time she was the most powerful vessel afloat and rendered practically every other battleship in the world obsolete.*

LEFT: *In May 1906 the navy lost one of its most modern battleships, the* Montagu, *when she ran aground in fog off Lundy Island. Completed in October 1903 the* Montagu *belonged to the* Duncan *class and formed part of the Mediterranean Fleet until January 1905 when she joined the Channel Fleet. The wreck was later broken up where it lay.*

RIGHT: *In December 1905 Henry Campbell-Bannerman, the leader of the Liberal Party, became Prime Minister. The Government at once began a series of social reforms which placed serious restrictions on the Service Estimates. They were committed, however, to carrying on with the Cawdor Programme of construction initiated by the previous Conservative Government. The accompanying illustration of Campbell-Bannerman was taken about 1888.*

LEFT: *Simultaneously with the construction of the* Dreadnought *a new type of vessel was under construction, built on very similar lines to the dreadnought type warship. This new type of vessel was to form a high speed squadron of warships to scout ahead of the main battle fleet. The illustration shows the* Inflexible *with the* Indomitable *behind.*

RIGHT: *The First Lord of the Admiralty under the Liberal Administration was Lord Tweedmouth who unfortunately suffered from ill health. Under pressure from the Prime Minister he was forced to make reductions in the planned programme of dreadnought construction.*

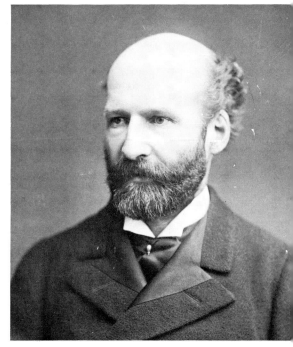

*Breakaway elements of the Navy League formed the
Imperial Maritime League in 1907 with the aim of
overthrowing the First Sea Lord, Admiral Fisher. On
February 6, 1908,* The Times *published a letter from
Viscount Esher to the Maritime League in which was
included a statement to the effect that the whole of the
German Empire would welcome the removal of Admiral
Fisher. The Kaiser at once wrote a personal letter to the
First Lord, Lord Tweedmouth, questioning the apparent
British fear of the growth of the German Navy, as he had
no wish to challenge the might of the Royal Navy. Lord
Tweedmouth in a personal reply to the Kaiser on February
20, included details of the forthcoming Navy Estimates. The
letter was sent with the full approval of the Foreign
Secretary, but unfortunately before the Estimates had been
put before the British Government. On March 9, 1908,
Lord Tweedmouth was called before the House of Lords to
explain his actions and the accompanying illustration shows
him* (standing) *answering questions.*

The last group of dreadnoughts ordered by the Conservatives before they were defeated in the General Election of December 1905 was the Bellerophon *class*. *The photograph shows the* nameship *of the class*.

In the *1907–1908* Estimates the Admiralty ordered the St. Vincent *class of dreadnoughts. These vessels, of which the illustration shows the* Vanguard *soon after completion, were practically repeats of the earlier* Bellerophon *class*.

303

LEFT: *In 1908 Herbert Henry Asquith* (left) *acceded to the post of Prime Minister on the death of Sir Henry Campbell-Bannerman.*

BELOW, LEFT: *With Asquith as Prime Minister, Lord Tweedmouth resigned his post as First Lord on the grounds of ill health. His place was taken by Reginald McKenna* (below, left) *who, with Lord Fisher to advise him, did much to prepare the Royal Navy for World War I.*

OPPOSITE, TOP: *The* Neptune, *shown here, was completed in 1911 and was the first British battleship to be fitted with a director tower for firing the guns in salvoes. This type of fitting had been recommended to the Admiralty some years previously by Sir Percy Scott, but the idea had not been taken up. The picture shows the* Neptune *early in the First World War after her fore funnel had been raised and six twin searchlights fitted on the bridge. The director is immediately below the control top on the foremast.*

OPPOSITE, RIGHT: *In August 1907 an expedition under Ernest Shackleton left England aboard the* Nimrod *in an attempt to reach the South Pole. After scaling Mount Erebus and locating the South Magnetic Pole they were forced to turn back, their goal unachieved. On their return to England the party was presented with medals by the King and some of them are seen here leaving Buckingham Palace after their investiture.*

The first two dreadnoughts laid down under the "We want Eight" Programme were the Colossus *and* Hercules. *Shown here just after completion, the* Colossus *clearly show the bad position of the foremast with its director behind the forefunnel.*

Following the trials of the battlecruiser Lion, *completed in 1912, certain modifications had to be made to the position of the funnel and the foremast. The boiler uptakes for the first funnel were raked aft so that the funnel could be sited behind the foremast instead of in front of it. This removed the menace of smoke fouling the vision of the fire control officer in the control position. In addition to this modification the bridge on top of the conning tower was moved behind it, and greatly enlarged. At the same time all three funnels were raised in height. The picture shows the* Lion *just after completion and before these modifications had been made.*

During the period when the dreadnought construction programme was at its height severe criticism was laid against Admiral Fisher by Admiral Lord Charles William de la Poer Beresford. The illustration shows Lord Beresford in the uniform of a Rear-Admiral.

307

ABOVE: *The accompanying illustration of the* Princess Royal *shows the new position of the foremast and fore funnel, and the new bridge arrangement.*

BELOW: *Under the 1908–1909 Estimates five protected cruisers of the* Bristol *class were ordered as a reply to the small cruisers then under construction for the German Navy. The picture below is of the* Bristol.

ABOVE: *Between 1906 and 1909 twelve destroyers of the* Tribal *class were completed. These vessels were of a much superior design, and the* Amazon *is shown here on trials in 1907.*

BELOW: *The* Tribal *class destroyers were followed by sixteen vessels of the* Beagle *class. The illustration shows the* Nautilus *completing at the Thames Iron Works in 1910. In 1913 she was renamed the* Grampus.

LEFT: *With the Beresford-Fisher feud at its height Commander Bacon of the Mediterranean Fleet sent a series of letters to Admiral Fisher commenting on the poor state of readiness of the Mediterranean Fleet. Unfortunately the letters fell into the hands of some of Lord Beresford's supporters and they were published. As a result of this Lord Fisher was forced to resign from the Admiralty. The illustration shows Commander Bacon as Second-in-Command to Captain Charles Campbell of the Theseus.*

ABOVE: *When Admiral Fisher resigned as First Sea Lord he was succeeded by Admiral of the Fleet, Sir Arthur Knyvet (Tug) Wilson. Sir Arthur Wilson had been Admiral Fisher's right hand man at the Admiralty and continued the policies begun by Admiral Fisher.*

BELOW: *The accompanying illustration shows the submarine D1 experimentally fitted with the new form of communication—wireless telegraphy.*

RIGHT: *Following the Agadir crisis the Prime Minister decided that the First Lord of the Admiralty and the Chancellor of the Exchequer should exchange posts. Thus in October 1911 Winston Leonard Spencer Churchill became the First Lord of the Admiralty. Prince Louis of Battenberg was appointed as First Sea Lord of the Admiralty. Churchill at once began a complete reorganisation of the Royal Navy and its defences. The picture shows the First Lord and First Sea Lord arriving at Dover in 1911 to inspect the new naval harbour.*

BELOW: *In the illustration the Battle Cruiser Squadron is shown at Scapa Flow in 1912. The vessels are, reading from left to right:* Indefatigable, Invincible, Inflexible *and* Indomitable.

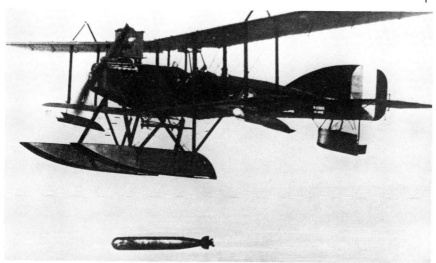

OPPOSITE, TOP: *Continuing his inspections of Admiralty establishments the First Lord visited the training ship* Mercury *in 1912, where he found the cadets lined up in bare feet on the grass of the base.*

OPPOSITE, LEFT: *In 1912 a new branch of the Royal Navy was formed. This was the aircraft wing. One of the first aircraft to be operated by the new branch was the Sopwith Tabloid which was first demonstrated in 1913. The picture is of one of the earliest production models.*

TOP: *The real value of the aircraft as a weapon of war for the navy was first demonstrated in July 1914 when a Short Type 184 seaplane dropped a 14in Whitehead torpedo of 810lb from the air. The illustration shows a Type 184 seaplane in the act of dropping such a torpedo.*

ABOVE: *Present at the Review in July 1914 were representatives of the new RNAS. The illustration shows the Short S.81 seaplane No. 126, which was a special aircraft supplied to the Naval Wing in 1913 for a series of experiments with 1½pdr guns, one of which can be seen mounted in the nose of the seaplane.*

The accompanying illustration shows the rangefinder on board the flagship Iron Duke. *To the left can be seen an anti-aircraft gun behind the wire netting which protects the wireless aerials.*

In July 1914 the Grand Fleet assembled at Portland for a Review by His Majesty, King George V. The illustration shows the Royal Yacht Alexandra *with the King on board passing the battlecruiser* New Zealand.

Following the Review the Grand Fleet put to sea for exercises before dispersing to its bases.

The Commander-in-Chief of the Grand Fleet, Admiral Sir George Callaghan proceeded to Scapa Flow by land, in order to have consultations at the Admiralty concerning the political situation.

The First Lord of the Admiralty, however, felt that Sir George Callaghan was not quite the right man to lead the navy in the forthcoming war, and on the grounds that the Admiral's health would not stand the strain of a long war, Churchill replaced him by Admiral John Rushworth Jellicoe, shown above in 1914.